"WE PULL
CODE AP
TOGETHER" —Dan Rostenkowski

Where does this revolutionary tax act leave you?
Your job, savings, retirement benefits? Will you be
one of the millions to benefit from tax savings ...
or need to act *now* to safeguard your income and
capital?

Do you know:

—About the 5% surcharge that appears in the new
tax law's fine print?

—That if you pay sales tax, the new tax law will
cost you *hundreds of dollars in lost deductions*?

—About the *increased* rates (and preferences) for
the Alternative Minimum Tax?

—That even though the interest payments on your
home are still deductible, interest on a
homeowner's loan may not be?

—Twenty percent of the cost of business
entertainment is now not deductible?

—How you can still contribute to an IRA?

—That your allowable contribution to a deferred
savings plan has been cut by 76.6%?

What the New Tax Law Means to You, from the
J.K. Lasser Tax Institute, is the one book that can
answer these questions ... and many more.

J.K. Lasser's

WHAT THE NEW TAX LAW MEANS TO YOU

A joint project of
The J.K. Lasser Tax Institute
Prentice-Hall Information Services

PUBLISHED BY POCKET BOOKS NEW YORK

POCKET BOOKS, a division of Simon & Schuster, Inc.
1230 Avenue of the Americas, New York, N.Y. 10020

ISBN: 0-671-63805-X

First Pocket Books printing October, 1986

10 9

POCKET and colophon are registered trademarks of Simon & Schuster, Inc.

Printed in the U.S.A.

CONTENTS

The 1986 Tax Reform Act is unprecedented in the depth and range of its sweeping changes. With the President's signature on the law, gone will be such long established tax features as multi-tax brackets, long-term capital gain breaks, income averaging, the dividend exclusion, unlimited family income-splitting advantages and tax shelter writeoffs. The Act presents you with new challenges to reduce your taxes and conserve capital. Although the effect of the Act will take some years to assess, right now you must alert yourself to its radical changes and integrate them into your financial decisions.

To help you do this, we have prepared J.K. Lasser's *What the New Tax Law Means to You*, which explains and analyzes the Act and tells you what steps you should take before the end of 1986 and afterwards.

We are grateful to Julian Block, of Prentice-Hall Information Services, who wrote this book under nearly impossible circumstances.

1
YOUR GUIDE TO THE NEW TAX LAWS

The Tax Reform Act of 1986 restructures the Internal Revenue Code from top to bottom. This historic legislation makes sweeping changes in the Federal income tax laws, the most far-reaching since World War II. Those revisions do something for, or to, nearly every household and business in the nation. The legislation cuts tax rates for individuals and corporations and also ends or restricts a vast array of deductions and other tax breaks.

This book gives you clear, uncomplicated and immediately helpful explanations of the most significant changes. First, though, here is a guide to the new law that summarizes the highlights of the key provisions.

Individual tax rate reductions. The centerpiece of the tax overhaul legislation is the lowering of the tax rates for individuals, generally to take effect in 1988. The Tax Reform Act reduces the top rate from 50% to 28%, with a rate of 33% for individuals with taxable incomes above certain levels. When combined with increased personal exemptions and standard deductions, the decreased rates will allow *most* individuals to enjoy a drop in their tax bills. Others, however, are going to end up with an overall hike in their taxes.

The new law scraps the current 15 brackets that start at 11% and go as high as 50%. For 1988, there are two brackets of 15% and 28%.

For 1987, the rates are blended, which means that they are a mix of the old and new rates. The rate structure consists of five brackets that start at 11% and peak at 38.5%. Beginning in 1989, after the new rate system is fully in place, the rates are adjusted annually to offset the effects of inflation. See chapter 2 for a detailed discussion of rate reductions.

Standard deduction increased. The new law increases the flat standard deduction for persons who do not itemize. The current deduction of $3,670 for joint filers and $2,480 for singles jumps to $5,000 for joint filers and $3,000 for singles. That change, though, does not take effect until 1988. For 1987, the amounts are $3,760 for joint filers and $2,540 for singles. Starting in 1989, the standard deduction figures are adjusted for inflation.

There are different and more generous rules for the elderly (age 65 or older) and the blind. Beginning in 1987, they may use the higher 1988 standard deduction figures of $3,000 or $5,000. Also, a joint filer who is elderly or blind is entitled to an extra standard deduction of $600

($1,200 if both spouses are elderly or blind, or one mate is elderly and the other one is blind). A single person who is elderly or blind gets an extra standard deduction of $750 ($1,500 for someone who is both elderly and blind). The extra standard deduction is in addition to the full standard deduction of $5,000 or $3,000.

Other new and complicated rules restrict the standard deduction for children. These rules apply to a child who has investment earnings and can be claimed as a dependent by a parent.

See chapter 2 for more details on the overhaul of the standard deduction.

Personal exemptions. The Tax Reform Act increases the personal exemptions that you claim for yourself, your spouse and your dependents. The current exemption figure of $1,080 becomes $1,900 in 1987, $1,950 in 1988 and $2,000 in 1989. Beginning in 1990, the personal exemption amount is adjusted for inflation.

Older individuals are no longer going to be allowed to claim extra exemptions for being age 65 or over. Nor can blind persons claim extra exemptions. However, as explained above, elderly and blind individuals who are not itemizers get extra standard deductions.

There is also bad news for high-income individuals. Beginning in 1988, there is a phasing out of personal exemptions for individuals with taxable incomes above certain levels. Those levels are $149,250 for joint filers and $89,560 for single filers.

Another change eliminates deductions claimed by dependent children on their own returns. The law now allows a double benefit: The exemption for a child can be claimed by a parent or other family member on that person's Form 1040 and by the child on the child's own Form 1040. Beginning in 1987, the revised rules prohibit an exemption for a child on the child's return when he or she can be claimed on someone else's return. See chapter 3 for more on the personal exemption increase.

Yet another tightening of the law may require you to get a Social Security number for your child. Starting with returns for 1987 to be filed in 1988, a person claiming a dependent who is at least five years old has to include the dependent's Social Security number on the return. Chapter 13 explains this requirement.

There will be less shelter for a child's investment earnings. In 1986, your dependent child can use his $1,080 personal exemption to shelter his investment earnings. After 1986, as explained above, your child has no personal exemption because you will claim him on your return. The new law, however, provides some relief. Starting in 1987, unlike earlier years, your child can use up to $500 of his standard deduction to offset investment earnings. That, of course, leaves only $2,040 (full standard deduction in 1987 for a single person of $2,540 minus $500) to shelter his wages from jobs. See chapter 5 for the new rules on taxing children's income.

Deduction for working couples. The Tax Reform Act abolishes the deduction for two-paycheck couples after 1986. Current law allows a couple to deduct 10% of the lower paid spouse's earnings, for a top deduction of $3,000. See chapter 3.

Income averaging. After 1986, individuals can no longer use averaging to reduce their taxes. See chapter 2.

Itemized deductions. Several popular personal deductions survived the Tax Reform Act relatively unscathed. There is no decrease in the itemized deductions you are entitled to claim for charitable contributions, real estate taxes and state and local income and property taxes. Other deductions, though, were ended or curtailed by the tax legislation.

Charitable contributions. The next few months are a good time to make charitable contributions. Why? Because the new law cuts tax rates, starting in 1987. By accelerating your charitable contributions, you are offsetting higher-taxed

1986 income, instead of lower-taxed 1987 income.

Tax strategy. It's also a wise maneuver for nonitemizers to make 1986 a big year for their charitable contributions. The charitable deduction for nonitemizers goes off the books after 1986, as scheduled. Congress refused to extend this break for nonitemizers.

Tax strategy. Whether you are an itemizer or a nonitemizer, don't overlook this year-end maneuver. You can mail a donation check as late as December 31 and still deduct it in 1986. Even better: Charge the contribution on your credit card and deduct it in 1986—even though the credit card bill is not paid until 1987.

Tax strategy. One particularly effective way to make a contribution in 1986 is to donate property that has appreciated in value—specifically, stocks or other investments that would have produced long-term capital gains if sold. Why? Because, as a general rule, you can deduct the full market value of the investment. So you are getting a deduction for appreciation in value, without being taxed on the gain. On the other hand, had you sold the property, 40% of your long-term gain would count as reportable income. And if you contributed the after-tax proceeds, you would have a smaller contribution—and a smaller deduction.

What if you contribute appreciated property after 1986? Starting in 1987, the untaxed portion of a donation of appreciated property is considered a "tax preference item" for purposes of the alternative minimum tax on individuals. Consequently, a donation of appreciated property after 1986 increases your chances of getting hit with the alternative minimum tax if you have a relatively low regular tax bill. See chapter 2 for a discussion of the minimum tax.

State and local sales taxes. The deduction for state and local sales taxes ends after 1986.

Tax strategy. Planning to purchase a car or some other big-ticket item in the near future? Do it before the close of 1986, while you are still able to take advantage of the deduction.

Sales taxes for which a deduction is not allowable, but which are allocated to a property purchase, are added to the property's basis. See chapter 3.

Medical expenses. For 1986, unreimbursed medical expenses are deductible to the extent that they exceed 5% of your adjusted gross income. Beginning in 1987, the nondeductible floor becomes 7.5%. See chapter 3.

> **Tax strategy.** Does someone in your family have elective surgery coming up? It may be deductible if performed in 1986, but nondeductible if performed in 1987.

Interest. After 1986, interest paid on consumer debt (for instance, car loans and credit charges) is not fully deductible. That includes interest on tax underpayments (except deferred estate taxes). Interest on debt incurred for investment reasons can be written off only up to the amount of your investment income. The cutback for both kinds of interest is phased in over five years: 35% disallowed in 1987, 60% in 1988, 80% in 1989, 90% in 1990 and 100% in 1991 and thereafter.

There is a key exception for mortgage interest. You can continue to deduct it for the purchase of up to two residences. However, mortgage interest on the part of a loan made after August 16, 1986 that exceeds the original purchase price of a home, plus any improvements, is not deductible, unless the loan proceeds are used for medical or educational purposes. See chapter 3.

Adoption expenses. This deduction is repealed after 1986. See chapter 3.

Housing allowances for ministers and military personnel. Mortgage interest and real estate taxes allocable to tax-free allowances for ministers and military personnel are deductible. See chapter 3.

Casualty losses. No deduction for a loss on personal property to the extent an insurance claim is not filed. A casualty loss deduction becomes available for deposits lost in bank failures. See chapter 3.

Moving expenses. For 1986, the deduction for job-related moving expenses is an "above-the-line" adjustment. That means the moving-expense deduction is a subtraction from gross income to arrive at adjusted gross income that is deductible by taxpayers who take the standard deduction, as well as those who itemize. Beginning in 1987, it can be taken only by itemizers. See chapter 3 for more on moving expenses.

Employee business expenses. In general, unreimbursed employee business expenses (including travel and entertainment and expenses of outside salespersons, previously deductible as above-the-line adjustments) are combined with most miscellaneous itemized deductions (including investment-connected expenses, such as stock market publications, and fees paid to return preparers). Starting in 1987, total miscellaneous expenses are deductible only to the extent that they exceed 2% of adjusted gross income. See chapter 3.

> **Tax strategy.** Take as many miscellaneous itemized deductions as you can this year. These include professional dues, investment magazine subscriptions, safe deposit fees, resumes, etc.

Home-office expenses. After 1986, they are limited to your net income from the business (gross income minus deductions attributable to the business). See chapter 3.

Hobby losses. Under the hobby loss rules, losses are deductible only to the extent of hobby income. Starting in 1987, it's possible to sidestep these rules if an activity is profitable in three out of five (instead of two out of five) consecutive years. The Tax Act leaves unchanged the two-out-of-seven-years rule for horse breeding activities. See chapter 3.

Business meals and entertainment/travel expenses. The Tax Reform Act makes sweeping changes, beginning in 1987. As a general rule, the Act limits the deduction for business meals and entertainment to 80% of their cost. "Quiet business meals" are no longer deductible. You must discuss business before, during or after the meal. Deductions for tickets to entertainment events generally cannot exceed the cost of regular tickets and are subject to the 20% disallowance rule. Deductions for renting luxury skyboxes at sports arenas are disallowed (phased out over three years) to the extent they are in excess of the cost of regular tickets when the skyboxes are used for more than one event. Travel expenses for what the law refers to as luxury water travel are generally limited to twice the highest Federal government travel allowance rate times the number of days in transit. See chapter 10.

Starting in 1987, the cost of attending investment-related seminars and conferences becomes nondeductible, as does travel as a form of education and travel on behalf of charitable organizations, "unless no significant amount of personal pleasure is involved." In general, unreimbursed employee travel and entertainment expenses, including those of outside salespersons (previously deductible as subtractions from gross income to arrive at adjusted gross income) are combined with most miscellaneous itemized deductions. The total expenses are allowable only to the extent that they exceed 2% of adjusted gross income. See chapter 3.

Individual retirement accounts. The Tax Reform Act generally retains the existing rules for persons without employee retirement plans. They can continue to deduct IRA contributions of up to $2,000 each year. But beginning in 1987, there are restrictions on deductions for individuals with retirement plans. The deduction phases out between $40,000 and $50,000 of adjusted gross income for joint filers if either spouse has a retirement plan and between $25,000 and $35,000 for singles. Individuals who are no longer eligible to make deductible contributions are still allowed to make *nondeductible* contributions and defer taxes on the earnings from such contributions until withdrawals start. See chapter 8.

Tax strategy. Make your 1986 IRA contributions up to April 15, 1987, and contribute the maximum amount.

Lump-sum withdrawals from retirement plans. The Tax Reform Act curbs special averaging breaks available to individuals who take lump-sum withdrawals from their retirement plans. The restrictions apply to withdrawals made after 1986. See chapter 8.

401(k) plans. Beginning in 1987, 401(k) plans become subject to a $7,000 cap. See chapter 8.

> **Tax strategy.** The currently allowable maximum deferral limitation is $30,000. Consider maximizing contributions to your 401(k) plan before the January 1, 1987 effective date of the new law.

Three-year recovery of cost rule. The Tax Reform Act repeals a special "three-year cost recovery rule" that relieves many retired government employees of taxes on pension benefits received during the first three years of their retirement until they recover all of their own contributions. The repeal is retroactive to July 1, 1986. See chapter 8.

Exclusions from income. The Tax Reform Act repeals or restricts tax-free treatment for several kinds of income. These changes are covered in chapter 4. They are:

(1) Unemployment compensation becomes fully taxable after 1986.

(2) Scholarships and fellowships granted to degree candidates after August 16, 1986, stay free of taxes only for amounts spent on tuition and course-required equipment. Starting with 1987 returns filed in 1988, there is no tax break for scholarship dollars spent on room and board or incidental expenses, such as travel, research, clerical help or equipment. Also repealed is tax-free treatment for payments for research or teaching required of all candidates for a particular degree or for recipients of certain federal grants.

(3) Tax-free treatment ends after 1986 for certain prizes and awards granted for achievement in fields such as the arts or sciences. To avoid taxes on the award, the recipient must assign the proceeds to charity.

(4) The exclusion for income earned abroad by U.S. citizens drops from $80,000 to $70,000, beginning in 1987.

(5) The Act clarifies the taxability of employee awards received from employers for length of service and safety achievement, and the deductibility by employers of those awards. See chapter 9.

Income shifting. Perhaps the simplest way for parents to shift income is to give income-producing property to their children. Generally, the Tax Reform Act restricts the benefit of shifting income to children under the age of 14.

After 1986, investment earnings above $1,000 for a child under 14 are, in most cases, taxed at the tax rate of a parent. It makes no difference whether the earnings came from money or other assets given to the child by a parent or by someone other than a parent—for instance, a grandparent. Nor does it matter that such gifts were made before 1987. If the child is 14 or over, earnings continue to be taxed at the child's rate.

Also, the Act essentially ends the shifting of income through temporary trust arrangements that usually run no more than ten years. Under the new rules, the trust income is generally taxed to the person who puts income-generating property into these trusts, often referred to as "Clifford" or "short-term" trusts. See chapter 5 for a detailed discussion of the effect of the new rules on income shifting between parents and children.

Capital gains. The Act ends the preferential treatment for long-term capital gains. Currently, the top rate on capital gains for individuals is 20%. Starting in 1987, capital gains are taxed at the same rate as other income, subject to a top rate of 28%. Capital losses will be allowed in full against capital gains and $3,000 of other income.

The capital gains rate for corporations goes from 28% to 34%. See chapter 6 for capital gains rules for individuals and chapter 11 for tax rates for corporations.

Crackdown on tax shelter losses. A tough set of rules introduced by the Tax Reform Act prevents you from using a loss from a "passive activity" (a business or investment in which you do not materially participate or are not involved in on a regular, continuous and substantial basis) to shelter your "active income" (salary, for example) or "portfolio income" (dividends, interest and capital gains). You are allowed to write off a tax shelter loss only against other tax shelter income.

What if you have no other current tax shelter income? Your loss is carried over to offset tax shelter income in future years. If you have yet to use up the loss by the time you sell the investment, it is offset against your otherwise taxable gain on the sale.

The crackdown takes effect gradually over a five-year period. In 1987, investors can write off 65% of tax shelter losses against non-tax shelter income. In 1988, only 40% can be written off. In 1989 and 1990, writeoffs are limited to 20% and 10%, respectively. The crackdown is fully in place starting in 1991. Important: The new rules apply to losses incurred in these years even though you may have invested in the shelter before 1987.

There are exceptions for three kinds of tax shelters. Losses or credits from these shelters can be used, within limits, to offset income from any source, including salary and portfolio income.

Rental real estate. The first $25,000 of loss can be used to offset income from any source. To qualify, you must "actively participate" in the management and operation of the property and have an annual adjusted gross income of under $100,000. There is a phase-out for adjusted gross income between $100,000 and $150,000 (without any reduction for passive-activity losses).

Tax credits for rehabilitating certain types of buildings and constructing and rehabilitating low-income housing. These credits can be used to offset up to $25,000 of income from any source. There is a phase-out for adjusted gross income between $200,000 and $250,000 (without any reduction for passive-activity losses). In general, the credits for low-income housing can be taken only for property placed in service before 1990.

"Working interests" in oil and gas drilling operations. These interests are completely exempt from the crackdown. They are fully deductible against any income. A "working interest" generally means a higher degree of personal liability than is usually found in the typical oil or gas limited partnership. For example, if there is an explosion at the drill site, a "working interest" might require you to lay out more cash, over and above the amount of your initial investment. See chapter 7 for a more detailed discussion of the new restrictions for shelter losses.

At-risk rules. The Tax Reform Act brings real estate acquired after 1986 under the restrictions imposed by the so-called at-risk rules. These rules limit the loss writeoff on an investment to the amount "at risk"—generally, the cash invested plus borrowed amounts on which the investor is personally liable (recourse loans). There is an exception from the at-risk rules for real estate bought with certain third party nonrecourse (no personal liability) financing. See chapter 7.

Rehabilitation tax credit. The new law reduces, but does not eliminate, the credit for rehabilitating certain types of buildings. After 1986, as a general rule, there are only two credits. One is a 20% credit for historic structures. The other is a 10% credit for industrial and commercial properties built before 1936. See chapter 7.

Low-income housing. There are three separate credits for (1) new construction and rehabilitation of existing housing; (2) certain federally subsidized new construction and rehabilitation; and (3) acquisition of existing housing. See chapter 7.

Depreciation deductions and investment credit.
The Tax Reform Act repeals the investment
credit as of the start of 1986. It generally retains
the basic ACRS system, but with modifications
for property placed in service after December 31,
1986. But you can elect to use either the old or
the new depreciation rules for property placed in
service after July 31, 1986 and before December
31, 1986. Under the new rules, there is a five-
year, instead of three-year, recovery period for
some equipment, such as cars. For most equipment, the recovery periods are five or seven
years. For real estate, the depreciation periods
are lengthened from 19 years to 27½ years for
residential rental property and 31½ years for
commercial property. The first-year expensing
deduction goes from $5,000 to $10,000, with a
phasing out for equipment purchases above
$200,000. See chapter 12.

Alternative minimum tax. The Tax Reform
Act establishes tougher minimum tax rules for
both individuals and corporations. The new
rules apply after 1986.

Individuals. The alternative minimum tax generally applies to high-income persons with large
amounts of what the law refers to as "preference
items." These tax-preference items are added to
the taxpayer's regular income, certain special exemptions and deductions are subtracted, and the

alternative minimum tax rate is applied to the net amount. If the alternative minimum tax bill exceeds the taxpayer's regular tax bill, the alternative tax becomes due.

The new legislation retains the basic structure, but with modifications. The tax rate increases from 20% to 21%. There is no change in the exemption amount of $40,000 for joint filers and $30,000 for singles. The exemption, however, is phased out to the extent that alternative minimum taxable income exceeds $150,000 for joint filers and $112,500 for singles.

The expanded list of preference items for both individuals and corporations includes untaxed appreciation on charitable contributions of property and interest on most municipal bonds issued for nonessential functions after August 7, 1986. In general, though, municipal bond interest remains exempt from the alternative minimum tax, as well as from the regular income tax. See chapter 2 for a detailed discussion of the alternative minimum tax for individuals.

Corporations. The Act replaces the add-on minimum tax with an alternative minimum tax similar to that for individuals. The corporate rate is 20%. The exemption of $40,000 phases out between $150,000 and $310,000 of alternative minimum taxable income.

The expanded list of corporate preferences includes an amount equal to 50% of the difference between book income (income figures used in financial reports) and taxable income for minimum tax purposes. After 1989, the use of book income to determine untaxed income is scheduled to be replaced by the use of earnings and profits under revised rules for determining earnings and profits. Chapter 11 discusses the alternative minimum tax for corporations.

Withholding and estimated taxes. The Tax Reform Act mandates changes in the tables used by employers to calculate how much to take out for taxes from the wages of their employees. Other changes affect the estimated taxes of many individual taxpayers. Here is a brief withholding and estimated tax calendar for 1986-1988:

No later than December 1, 1986: Employees should consider filing a new Form W-4 to take effect on January 1, 1987. They should increase or decrease their withholding to reflect changes put on the books by the new legislation that takes effect in 1987—for example, the loss of deductions for sales taxes and medical expenses.

January 1, 1987: Employers have to put new withholding tables into effect for wages paid after 1986. These tables take into account the blended (mix of the old and new rates) tax rate schedules for 1987.

April 15, 1987: This is the deadline for individuals required to make estimated payments to make their first payment for 1987 under new rules introduced by the Tax Reform Act.

Key change. Before 1987, individuals could avoid underpayment penalties if their quarterly estimated payments equaled at (1) 80% of their current year's tax bill or (2) 100% of their prior year's liability. The new law lifts the 80% figure to 90%, starting in 1987. It leaves unchanged the 100% escape hatch.

September 30, 1987: Employees are required to file revised W-4 Forms by this date. The forms are supposed to have been revised by then to take into account changes made by the Tax Act. Also, new withholding tables take effect on this date. Those tables will reflect the new tax rate schedules that become fully implemented in 1988. See chapter 13 for more details on withholding and estimated taxes.

Corporate tax rates decreased. The top rate becomes 34% for taxable years beginning after July 1, 1987. There are graduated rates of 15% and 25% for the first $75,000 of taxable income. The graduated rates phase out for taxable income between $100,000 and $335,000, so corporations pay a flat rate of 34% on taxable income beyond $335,000. See chapter 11.

Limitation on business tax credits. The limit on the amount of income tax liability that can be offset by business tax credits drops from 85% to 75% for taxable years that begin after 1985. Credits subject to the limitation include the research and development credit and the low-income housing credit. See chapter 11.

Research and development credit. The credit is extended for three years at a reduced rate of 20%. See chapter 12.

Stock redemption payments. After February 28, 1986, no deduction for payments by a corporation to redeem its stock, including "greenmail" payments to avoid an unfriendly takeover. See chapter 11.

Installment sale reporting restricted. In general, the Tax Reform Act ends installment reporting for (1) sales under a revolving credit plan, (2) sales of stocks and other publicly traded property, and (3) sales by certain dealers in property. See chapter 12.

Taxable years of partnerships, S corporations and personal service corporations. As a general rule, they now must be on a calendar year basis. See chapter 12.

2

PERSONAL TAX RATE REDUCTIONS

WHAT YOU SHOULD KNOW ABOUT TAX RATE REDUCTIONS

The 1986 Tax Reform Act scraps the old tax rate schedules and introduces completely new schedules. The new rates apply starting with returns for 1987 to be filed in 1988. The old rates remain applicable to returns for 1986 to be filed in 1987. All tax rate schedules may be found in the appendices at the end of this book.

Under prior law, individuals were taxed in as many as 15 brackets, according to their taxable income and filing status. The old rates began at 11% and went as high as 50%.

Officially, there are only two rates for 1988— 15% and 28%. Actually, tucked into the fine print is a third, higher rate of 33% for individuals with taxable incomes above certain levels.

The new law includes a number of special provisions that take tax benefits away from high-income individuals. One of them is a 5% surcharge or additional tax. This 5% surcharge phases out, that is, reduces the benefit that those with high incomes derive from the 15% rate. Also, there is a separate 5% surcharge that phases out the benefits of their personal exemptions.

Consider, for example, a married couple who file jointly in 1988. They are taxed at a 15% rate on their first $29,750 of taxable income and at a 28% rate on taxable income above $29,750. (Under the new rules, a person's taxable income equals adjusted gross income minus personal exemptions and minus either the standard deduction, which replaces the zero bracket amount, or the total of itemized deductions). The first surcharge applies to the couple's taxable income between $71,900 and $149,250. Their rate becomes 33% because, in effect, that surcharge works out to an extra 13% tax on the couple's first $29,750 of taxable income. As for the second surcharge, it kicks in only if taxable income exceeds $149,250. In that event, the effect of the second surcharge is to continue the 33% rate until the couple pays an extra $546 for each exemption that they claim. Once that happens, the top tax rate again becomes 28% for all additional taxable income.

In the case of a single person, the first surcharge causes the rate to become 33% for taxable income between $43,150 and $89,560. The second surcharge kicks in only if taxable income exceeds $89,560.

NOTE: The tax rates for 1988 are indexed, that is, adjusted annually to reflect inflation, starting with returns for 1989 to be filed in 1990.

For 1987, the rates are blended. That means they are determined under tables reflecting the new rates as of March 1987. The rates range from 11% to 38.5%, without any surcharges.

STANDARD DEDUCTION INCREASED

The new law replaces the zero bracket amount with the standard deduction, starting with returns for 1987 to be filed in 1988. The standard deduction amounts for 1987 are increased for 1988. Moreover, those amounts are indexed, that is, adjusted annually to reflect inflation, starting in 1989.

The standard deduction amounts for taxpayers who do not itemize (other than the elderly and blind; their amounts are higher, as explained below) are:

Filing Status	1987	1988
Marrieds filing jointly and surviving spouses	$3,760	$5,000
Heads of households	$2,540	$4,400
Unmarried individuals	$2,540	$3,000
Married filing separately	$1,900	$2,500

Elderly and blind. The elderly (age 65 or older) and blind can claim the higher 1988 standard deductions, starting in 1987. Also, beginning in 1987, the standard deduction amount for a single taxpayer who is age 65 or over or who is blind is increased by an additional standard deduction amount of $750 ($1,500 for someone who is both over 65 and blind). In the case of a married taxpayer who is age 65 or over or who is blind, the additional standard deduction amount is $600. Thus, the additional standard deduction amount becomes $1,200 if both spouses are blind or 65 or over, or one is age 65 or over and the other is blind.

Example. Scott and Zelda Thurber are both age 66. Their standard deduction for 1987 is $6,200 (the sum of $5,000 plus $1,200).

Example. Fred C. Dobbs is blind. His standard deduction for 1987 is $3,750 (the sum of $3,000 plus $750) if he is under age 65 or $4,500 (the sum of $3,000 plus $1,500) if he is over age 65.

Standard deduction for a dependent child. A child can use up to $500 of his or her standard deduction to offset income from investment earnings, such as dividends and interest. Investment earnings above $1,000 (in most cases) received by a child under the age of 14 are taxed at the parent's rate. See chapter 5 for a detailed discussion of the new rules for taxing children's income.

NOTE: The new law is considerably tougher than the old law. On a return for 1986, a dependent child is relieved of taxes on the first $1,080 of investment earnings. Also, the rates begin at 11% on investment earnings above $1,080.

Taxpayers ineligible for standard deduction. The standard deduction is zero for the following five categories:

(1) married taxpayers filing separately if either spouse itemizes deductions;

(2) nonresident aliens

(3) U.S. citizens with excludable income from U.S. possessions;

(4) individuals who file returns for periods of less than 12 months because of accounting period changes; and

(5) estates or trusts, common trust funds, or partnerships.

New definition of taxable income. The new law simplifies the calculation of an individual's tax liability. Beginning with returns for 1987, all that an individual has to do is subtract the applicable standard deduction amount from adjusted gross income (AGI) to determine taxable income. Under the rules for returns filed for 1986 and earlier years, the determination did not involve such a subtraction for the zero bracket amount

(ZBA). Here's a comparison of the old and new definitions of taxable income for purposes of computing tax liability:

Under prior law, a nonitemizer calculated AGI and then subtracted the charitable deduction for a nonitemizer and all personal exemptions to arrive at taxable income. Next, the nonitemizer went directly to a tax table (without a subtraction for the ZBA because the ZBA was incorporated in the table) to determine tax liability. Tax rates ranged from 11% to 50%.

Prior law imposed an additional step on someone who itemized. An itemizer had to first reduce itemized deductions by the applicable ZBA (to avoid getting twice the allowable ZBA) and then subtract the remaining itemized deductions and personal exemptions to arrive at taxable income. After that, just as a nonitemizer did, the itemizer went to a tax table.

Under the new law, a nonitemizer offsets AGI with the standard deduction (the Tax Act repealed the charitable deduction for nonitemizers) and personal exemptions to arrive at taxable income, before going to a tax table. An itemizer offsets AGI with itemized deductions and all personal exemptions to arrive at taxable income. Then, like a nonitemizer, the itemizer goes to a tax table.

Tax tables. As under prior law, Congress has authorized the Internal Revenue to prepare tax tables that reflect the tax liability of individuals who use the standard deduction, as well as tables for itemizers. Since the prior tables that incorporated the ZBA are replaced by tables that do not incorporate the standard deduction, the new tax law authorizes the IRS to adjust the size of the intervals between taxable income amounts in the new tables to reflect meaningful differences in tax liability.

PERSONAL EXEMPTIONS INCREASED

The new law raises the personal exemption for an individual, the individual's spouse, and each dependent to $1,900, starting with returns for 1987 to be filed in 1988. The exemption amount is raised to $1,950 for 1988 and $2,000 for 1989. The $2,000 amount is indexed, that is, adjusted for inflation, beginning with returns for 1990 to be filed in 1991.

Phase-out of exemption for individuals with taxable incomes above certain levels. Starting with returns for 1988 to be filed in 1989, the Tax Act phases out, that is, reduces the benefit derived from personal exemptions by individuals with taxable incomes above certain levels. The phase-out affects all exemptions that can be claimed on a return, including those for a spouse and dependents. It is one of a number of new measures enacted to limit the windfall that high-income individuals may reap from lower tax rates.

The mechanism for the phase-out is a 5% surcharge or additional tax. The surcharge applies only if taxable income exceeds $149,250, in the case of a married couple filing jointly, or $89,560, in the case of a single person. The surcharge remains applicable until the benefit of the exemptions totally phase out.

Starting with returns for 1989 to be filed in 1990, the $149,250 and $89,560 figures are indexed, that is, adjusted annually to reflect inflation. For more on the phase-out, see the earlier discussion in this chapter of tax rate reductions.

Elderly and the blind. The new law repeals the additional exemptions for the elderly and blind, starting with returns for 1987.

Note: The new law partially offsets the loss of these exemptions in the case of elderly and blind taxpayers who are not itemizers and use the standard deduction. As previously explained, the standard deduction amounts increase by $750 for a single taxpayer who is age 65 or over or who is blind and by $600 for a married taxpayer who is age 65 or over or who is blind.

Prohibition of exemption for dependent child. Under the new law, no exemption is allowed a child on his or her return when the child can be claimed as a dependent by the child's parent. It makes no difference that the parent does not actually claim the child.

This new restriction eliminates the double benefit allowed under the rules for returns filed for 1986 and earlier years. Under those rules, the exemption for a child could be claimed by a parent on the parent's return and by the child on his or her return.

Note: A related restriction concerns the standard deduction for a child who can be claimed as a dependent by a parent. That restriction is explained in the earlier discussion of standard deduction increases.

MINIMUM TAX WIDENDED

The alternative minimum tax (AMT) is designed to recoup benefits that have reduced or eliminated your regular income tax. AMT is imposed if it exceeds your regular income tax or if you have no tax liability after claiming certain tax deductions or credits. What that means is that you have to pay the AMT if your liability under AMT is greater than under the regular tax.

Under prior law, the AMT rate is a flat 20% applied to AMT taxable income (generally, adjusted gross income increased by tax preference items that are added back to income and decreased by certain itemized deductions) after claiming an exemption. The exemption is $40,000 for married couples filing jointly, $30,000 for unmarried persons or heads of household and $20,000 for married persons filing separately, trusts and estates. The resulting AMT is imposed to the extent it exceeds the regular income tax.

The AMT is retained by the 1986 Tax Reform Act, but with certain modifications that make it more potent. The new law requires taxpayers to add more preference items back to income in computing the AMT. The following changes apply to taxable years beginning after 1986.

Rate. The new rate is 21%.

Exemption amount. There is a phasing out of the exemption amount. It is reduced by 25% of the AMT taxable income in excess of $150,000 for joint returns, $75,000 for trusts, estates and marrieds filing separately and $112,500 for singles.

Tax preference items. The items listed below are tax preference items subject to AMT. However, you can elect to avoid AMT on some expense preferences.

● **Depreciation.** The new rules apply to accelerated depreciation on all property placed in service after 1986, other than property granted a transitional exception for regular tax depreciation and investment tax credit purposes. Accelerated depreciation is a preference to the extent it exceeds alternative depreciation as computed under the new rules. For property placed in service before 1987, prior law continues to apply.

● **Pollution control facilities.** Rapid amortization of these facilities is a preference, as was true under prior law. For facilities placed in service after 1986, taxpayers must use the alternative recovery system.

● **Completed contract method.** Taxpayers who use the completed contract method of accounting for long-term contracts entered into after March 1, 1986, for regular income tax purposes, must use the percentage of completion method on these contracts for AMT purposes.

● **Percentage depletion.** As was true under prior law, the preference item is the difference between claimed percentage depletion and the adjusted basis of the property at the end of the year, without regard to current depletion.

● **Intangible drilling costs.** The preference item is the excess of intangible drilling costs over 65% (rather than 100%, as under prior law) of net income from oil, gas and geothermal properties for the taxable year. Excess intangible drilling costs are those expenses in excess of the amount that would have been deducted had the expenses been either deducted ratably over ten years or deducted over the life of the well as cost depletion. Net income from oil, gas and geothermal properties is gross income (excluding rent or royalties paid to another for use of the property) reduced by deductions other than excess intangible drilling costs. Costs incurred in drilling a nonproductive well are not counted as a tax preference.

Note: The preference rule does not apply if you elect to deduct intangible drilling costs ratably over ten years.

● **Installment sales.** Taxpayers in the business of selling goods or real estate cannot use the installment method to defer AMT taxable income for taxable years beginning after 1986.

● **Mining exploration and development costs.** Costs paid or incurred after 1986 that are expensed for regular tax purposes are written off ratably over ten years for AMT purposes.

Note: The preference rule does not apply if you elect to deduct costs ratably over ten years.

● **Circulation and research and experimental expenditures.** Amounts paid or incurred by noncorporate taxpayers after 1986 that are deductible against the regular income tax must be deducted ratably over three years (circulation expenditures for newspapers, magazines and other periodicals) or over ten years (research and experimental expenditures) for AMT purposes. However, a special rule applies if the taxpayer incurs a loss on property that generates the circulation expenditures or a specific project generating research and experimental expenditures. In that event, all hitherto undeducted expenditures relating to the property are allowable as an AMT deduction for the loss year.

Note. The preference rule does not apply if you elect to deduct circulation expenses ratably over three years or research and experimental expenses ratably over ten years.

● **Tax exempt interest on nonessential function bonds.** A new preference item is interest on most municipal bonds issued for nonessential functions after August 7, 1986.

● **Charitable contributions of appreciated property.** A new preference item is the untaxed appreciation for a charitable contribution of property.

● **Incentive stock options.** As was true under prior law, exercise of an incentive stock option (see chapter 6 for a discussion of incentive stock options) produces a preference item. The amount is the excess of the fair market value of a share at the time of exercise over the option price. The market value is determined by considering only those restrictions that will never lapse.

● **Passive farm losses.** An individual's passive farm loss is generally a preference item. A passive farm loss is the loss incurred from a tax shelter farming activity. The preference amount is reduced by a taxpayer's insolvency (excess of liabilities over the fair market value of the assets).

A tax shelter farm activity may be a farming syndicate or any other farming activity where the taxpayer does not participate materially. There is material participation by a taxpayer when (1) the terms of the material participation standard for regular income tax purposes are met; (2) a family member participates; or (3) the taxpayer meets the requirements for treatment as a retired or disabled person or as a surviving spouse.

Deductions in excess of the gross income allocable to the passive farm loss activity are disallowed for AMT purposes. Each farm is generally treated as a separate activity.

Note: Income from one passive farming activity cannot be netted against other passive farming activity losses. A disallowed farming loss must be carried forward and netted against future income from the same activity, or until there is a disposition.

● **Passive activity losses.** The passive activity loss limitation (see chapter 7 for a discussion of passive losses) is identical for both regular tax and AMT purposes, with these three exceptions. First, the AMT rule is effective in 1987, whereas the regular tax rule is phased in over five years. Second, for AMT purposes, the disallowed loss amount is reduced by a taxpayer's insolvency (excess of liabilities over the market value of assets). Third, the AMT rules, including the passive farm loss rule, apply to the measurement and allowability of all relevant income, deduction, and credit items for limitation purposes.

The passive loss disallowance is determined after all preferences and adjustments have been computed, so the suspended loss amount may be different for AMT and regular tax purposes.

Itemized deductions. The new law leaves most AMT itemized deductions unchanged. Thus, the only itemized deductions allowable are those for: (1) casualty, theft and gambling losses; (2) charitable contributions; (3) medical expenses; (4) qualified interest; (5) the estate tax deduction for income in respect of a decedent; and (6) certain estate and trust distributions to beneficiaries. For a discussion of limitations on interest deductions, see chapter 3.

Note: State and local taxes are not deductible for AMT purposes. In a year in which you are subject to AMT, try to defer if possible the payment of such taxes to the next year. If you are subject to AMT, the payment of state and local taxes have no tax effect for Federal income tax purposes. By deferring payment to the year in which you are subject to regular income tax, you may then deduct the state and local payments.

Minimum tax credit. The AMT paid (that is, the net minimum tax) is allowable as a credit in subsequent years against the regular tax liability, net of the nonrefundable credits or the excess of the regular tax over the tentative minimum tax, if that is less than the regular tax. Thus, this credit, known as the minimum tax credit, cannot reduce taxes below the tentative minimum tax in a later year.

Unused credits can be carried over indefinitely, but cannot be carried back. They can be carried over as tax attributes in certain corporate acquisitions.

The year's minimum tax credit is, in general, composed of the aggregate post-1986 liability for AMT reduced by regular tax, to the extent it was not previously used as a credit. However, the minimum tax credit applies only to AMT liability incurred because of deferral preferences, such as depreciation, where the preference results from the timing rather than the amount of the deduction. So the minimum tax for this credit is reduced by the amount of AMT liability that would have been incurred if the only preferences were the exclusion preferences, which are percentage depletion and regular tax itemized deductions that are denied for AMT purposes.

Example: Al and Carol file a joint return with zero regular taxable income, $400,000 in deferral preferences, and $100,000 in exclusion preferences (including itemized deductions disallowed for AMT). With the 21% AMT rate and the phase-out of the exemption amount, the AMT would be $105,000 [21% × ($400,000 + $100,000 − $0)]. But if they had only exclusion preferences, the AMT liability would have been $12,600 [21% × ($100,000 − $40,000 exemption)]. So the minimum tax credit that can be used next year is $92,400 ($105,000 − $12,600).

Foreign tax credit. Special rules apply under the new law to the foreign tax credit. In general, the credit is allowable for AMT purposes under rules similar to those for individuals under prior law.

In the AMT formula, the credit against the tentative minimum tax is generally figured on the tax base against which the 21% rate is applied, while the regular tax reducing it is computed by using the regular foreign tax credit. The limitation on the amount of the credit must be applied separately for AMT and regular tax purposes, due to the difference between regular taxable income and AMT taxable income, in foreign tax applicable to them, and in the ratios of foreign taxable income to worldwide income. Taxpayers must also keep track of the respective foreign tax credit carryforwards allowable for both regular and AMT purposes.

When the foreign tax credit limitation is applied to the minimum tax rules and AMT taxable income is increased by a percentage of the excess of book income over AMT taxable income, the percentage of that income from sources within the United States will be treated the same as other U.S. source AMT taxable income. So the book income preference will not change the percentage that applies to the AMT foreign tax credit limitation.

Up to 90% of tentative minimum tax liability, before foreign tax credits, can be offset by foreign tax credits, even if, under the foreign tax credit limitation, more than 90% of the liability could be offset by the foreign tax credit. Foreign tax credits disallowed under this rule are treated, for carryover purposes, like credits disallowed under the foreign tax credit limitation. This rule is applied before comparing the minimum and regular tax liability amounts.

Incentive tax credits. Under prior law, taxpayers claimed nonrefundable credits (those that cannot exceed tax liability) against the regular tax even if they provided no benefit, that is, they reduced regular tax liability to less than the minimum tax liability. Where nonrefundable credits were not allowed against the AMT, these credits could be carried back or forward to other tax years.

In general, the new law does not allow taxpayers to claim such credits for the current year to the extent they reduce the regular tax liability to less than the tentative minimum tax liability, but unused credits can be carried back or forward to other tax years.

Note: Taxpayers are not required to file a form showing the minimum tax computation on account of this rule, if they owe no minimum tax and if the minimum tax does not limit the use of incentive credits.

Example. Alice King has a $100 regular tax liability (disregarding incentive credits), and a $10 targeted jobs tax credit. If her tentative minimum tax is less than $90, she would not have to file a minimum tax form.

Net operating losses. In general, the rules for net operating losses under the new law are the same as those under prior law for the AMT. The AMT net operating loss and carryovers are computed separately. The computation reflects the differences between the regular tax base and the

AMT base. A net operating loss may not offset more than 90% of AMT taxable income.

The net operating loss computation is the same for both regular tax and AMT purposes, with these two exceptions. First, the loss must be reduced by any deductions that are considered tax preference items. Second, only AMT itemized deductions may be claimed in figuring AMT taxable income.

For computing the loss in years other than the loss year, the recomputed loss is deducted from AMT taxable income, with certain modifications, in the carryover year, whether or not the taxpayer is subject to the minimum tax in that year.

There is a transition rule for corporations. It allows, for AMT purposes, all pre-effective date regular tax net operating losses to be carried forward as minimum tax net operating losses. They can be carried forward to the first tax year for which the tax, as amended under the new law, applies. Also, they can be carried forward until used up. Prior law remains applicable to individuals in calculating AMT net operating losses for such years.

Regular tax elections. For certain expenditures that would result in a tax preference if treated under the regular tax rules, taxpayers can elect to have the minimum tax rule for deducting the expenditure apply for regular tax purposes. This is known as a normative election that applies to the following expenditures:

Circulation expenditures

Research and experimental expenditures

Intangible drilling costs

Mining development and exploration expenditures

Taxpayers can make these elections on a "dollar-for-dollar" basis. Take, for example, a taxpayer who incurs intangible drilling costs of $100,000 on a particular well. The taxpayer can elect normative treatment for any portion of the $100,000. To the extent the election applies, no deduction is allowed either for regular or minimum tax purposes. And the election may be revoked only with consent of the IRS. Partners or shareholders of S corporations (corporations taxed like partnerships) can make the election separately for their allocable share of the expenditure.

Other rules. Besides the revisions discussed above, there are changes in the AMT rules. Corporations must make estimated tax payments for both minimum tax and regular tax purposes. Estates and trusts are allowed to take certain AMT itemized deductions. The IRS will issue regulations that explain how items treated for regular and minimum tax purposes are to be apportioned between the estate or trust and the beneficiaries.

There are rules on how to allocate items that are treated differently for regular and minimum tax purposes for common trust funds, regulated investment companies and real estate investment trusts, as well as on certain technical issues, such as short tax years and exemption amounts for consolidated returns. As under prior law, the IRS regulations will explain how to apply the tax benefit rule to items that are treated differently for regular and minimum tax purposes.

EARNED INCOME CREDIT INCREASED

The earned income credit provides a refund or subsidy for low income workers who have dependent children and maintain a household. In the case of a return for 1986, the maximum credit is $550.

The new law increases the credit from 11% to 14% of the first $5,714 of earned income, for a maximum credit of $800. On a return for 1987, the credit phases out beginning at an adjusted gross income (AGI) of $6,500 and phases out completely at an AGI or earnings of $14,500. Starting with returns for 1988, the phase-out begins at income of $9,000 and phases out completely at an AGI or earnings of $17,000.

Indexing for inflation. Starting in 1987, there are annual adjustments to reflect inflation in the earned income figure of $5,714 and the phase-out levels of $6,500 and $9,000.

INCOME AVERAGING REPEALED

The new law repeals income averaging, starting with returns for 1987 to be filed in 1988.

On returns for 1986 and earlier years, averaging saves taxes for an individual whose taxable income in the averaging year is $3,000 higher than 140% of his or her average taxable income for the previous three years.

3

PERSONAL DEDUCTIONS REPEALED OR RESTRICTED

RESTRICTIONS ON INTEREST DEDUCTIONS

The 1986 Tax Reform Act curtails or eliminates some of the itemized deductions previously available to individuals for interest payments on home mortgages and loans to finance investments or consumer purchases. The revised rules apply starting with returns for 1987 to be filed in 1988.

Interest on investment loans. Under the new law, there is a tighter limit on your annual deduction for payments of interest on borrowings to finance investments, such as margin accounts used to buy stocks. Previously, as a general rule, the law allowed you to deduct interest on investment loans up to the amount of $10,000, plus the amount that you receive as dividends, interest and other income from investments. Now, though, investment interest is deductible only to the extent of investment income.

Interest on consumer loans. The new rules also abolish deductions for interest payments on what the law calls "consumer loans." That means no deduction at all for interest on loans for things like cars, boats, charge account purchases, college tuition and so forth. To make things worse, the ban on consumer-interest deductions applies to interest paid on income taxes, other than interest on deferred payments of estate taxes.

Interest on home mortgages. The Tax Reform Act curtails somewhat the ability of taxpayers to circumvent the repeal of consumer-interest deductions. The law clamps some limits on deductions for interest on home mortgages.

The mortgage must be on a "principal home," which is legalese for a year-round place, or on a second home, like a country cottage. No deduction for mortgage interest is allowed on more than two dwellings.

Moreover, there is a complicated ceiling on the deduction allowed for interest payments on post-August 16th, 1986 mortgages. The ceiling is designed to stop a homeowner from negotiating a home-equity loan for the excess of "fair market value" over cost to increase interest writeoffs. As a general rule, mortgage interest is deductible only if the loans do not exceed the home's original purchase price plus the cost of any improvements. What if the loans exceed the cost-plus-improvements limit, but do not exceed the market value of the home? In that case, interest is deductible when the proceeds are used to cover educational or medical costs, but nondeductible when the proceeds cover other costs.

The deduction ceiling causes no problems as long as the loans are within the original cost-plus-improvements limit. All of the interest remains deductible. It makes no difference that a borrower spends nothing on home improvements and uses all of the loan proceeds to pay off existing loans or avoid new ones for cars and other consumer purchases—a maneuver likely to be employed by many tax-savvy homeowners burdened with consumer debts.

Nor is all necessarily lost when the loans exceed the original cost plus improvements, but not the market value of the home. As noted above, some relief remains available for loans backed up by the appreciated value of a home. To the extent the loans exceed the original cost-plus-improvements limit, but are within the market-value limit, the interest continues to be deductible when the borrower uses loan proceeds for educational or medical expenses.

To illustrate how these rules work, let's use the example of John and Virginia Hickey, who bought their home a number of years ago for $200,000. The Hickeys paid cash of $40,000 and assumed a mortgage of $160,000. Subsequently, John and Virginia spent $50,000 on home improvements and made mortgage payments that reduced their loan from $160,00 to $130,000. Nowadays, their home is valued at $300,000. The

Hickeys plan to refinance their dwelling or to tap their equity by taking out a home equity credit line secured by a second mortgage.

Under the new rules, there is a cap of $120,000 on the amount that the couple can borrow against their residence without running afoul of deduction restrictions. Why is their limit $120,000? Because that is the difference between $250,000 (the $200,000 original price, plus $50,000 improvements) and $130,000 (the unpaid mortgage on which interest is now being deducted). Homeowners like our hypothetical couple are absolutely free to spend their $120,000 on around-the-world cruises, stretch limos or whatever they crave, without suffering any loss of their interest deductions.

Now assume that the Hickeys raise their borrowings from $120,000 to $140,000 to pay for furniture or other "consumer purchases" like interest on hefty assessments of back taxes. With that set of facts, the couple forfeits their deduction for the interest on the additional $20,000.

Suppose, instead, that the Hickeys use the additional $20,000 to put their children through college or to pay medical bills. In that event, they keep their interest deduction.

NOTE: In calculating original purchase price of a first or second home, remember to include settlement or closing costs, such as title insurance and legal fees. As for improvements, count the cost of items that add to the value of a home, like paving a driveway and putting in new floors or plumbing, as opposed to outlays for routine repairs or maintenance that do not add to its value but merely keep it up, such as replacing a broken window pane or painting or papering a room. Note, too, that furniture, appliances and similar items that are not "fixtures" under the law where you live fail to qualify as part of a first or second dwelling.

NOTE: On pre-August 16, 1986 loans, you can continue to claim the full deduction on mortgage interest to the extent the loan does not exceed market value of the home at the time of the loan. It is immaterial that the loan exceeds the original purchase price, plus improvements.

The new rules apply to deductions for interest payments after 1986 on all loans, whether entered into before or after 1986. But the changes introduced by the Tax Act do not take full effect immediately. To cushion their immediate impact, they are phased in over a five-year period, not taking full effect until 1991. The Tax Act allows a deduction in 1987 for 65% of the otherwise nondeductible interest payments, 40% in 1988, 20% in 1989, 10% in 1990 and zero in 1991.

REPEAL OF DEDUCTION FOR SALES TAXES

The Tax Act repeals the itemized deduction for state and local sales taxes, starting with returns for 1987 to be filed in 1988.

Nondeductible taxes incurred to acquire or dispose of property. The new law specifies that where no itemized deduction is allowed for taxes incurred in a business or investment activity in connection with the acquisition or disposition of property, such taxes are to be treated as part of the cost of the acquired property or as a reduction in the amount realized on the disposition.

MEDICAL EXPENSE DEDUCTION CUTBACK

Starting with returns for 1987 to be filed in 1988, medical expenses are deductible only to the extent that their total exceeds 7.5% of a person's adjusted gross income for the year. Expenses below the 7.5% floor are nondeductible. Under the rules for returns for 1986, medical expenses are allowable only to the extent that their total exceeds 5% of a person's adjusted gross income.

Accommodating a personal residence to the needs of the handicapped. Congressional committee reports clarify the deductibility as a medical expense, subject to the 7.5% floor, of the full cost of certain home-related capital expenditures incurred by a physically handicapped individual to remove structural barriers in a personal residence so as to accommodate the handicapped condition. Qualifying costs include expenditures for these six categories as they do not add to the fair market value of a personal residence: (1) constructing entrance or exit ramps to the residence; (2) widening doorways at entrances or exits to the residence; (3) widening or otherwise modifying hallways and interior doorways to accommodate wheelchairs; (4) railing, support bars or other modifications to bathrooms to accommodate handicapped individuals; (5) lowering of or other modifications to kitchen cabinets and equipment to accommodate access by handicapped individuals; and (6) adjustment of electrical outlets and fixtures.

Why is this clarification by Congress significant? Because, as a general rule, the cost of medically related home improvements counts as a medical deduction only to the extent the outlay exceeds the increase in the home's value as a result of the improvement. Under the new law, the increase in the home's value as a result of qualifying improvements is deemed to be zero.

REPEAL OF DEDUCTION FOR ADOPTION EXPENSES

The Tax Act repeals the itemized deduction of up to $1,500 for adoption expenses for children with special needs and replaces it with an expansion of the Adoption Assistance Program under Title IV-E of the Social Security Act.

The new law applies, as a general rule, to expenses paid or incurred after 1986. However, prior law remains applicable to expenses paid or incurred during 1987 in connection with an adoption as to which the taxpayer paid or incurred expenses during 1986 that were deductible under prior law.

CHARITABLE DEDUCTION FOR NONITEMIZERS EXPIRES

Current law allows charitable deductions to be claimed by both itemizers and nonitemizers, subject to certain limits. The deduction for nonitemizers had been scheduled to expire after 1986. The Tax Reform Act allows the deduction for nonitemizers to expire as scheduled.

CHARITABLE DEDUCTION DENIED FOR CERTAIN TRAVEL

The Tax Reform Act ends deductions for "charitable" trips that are disguised vacations, starting with returns for 1987 to be filed in 1988. From now on, there are limitations on charitable deductions for travel expenses (including meals and lodging) incurred by volunteer workers who perform services away from their homes on behalf of charities. The deductions are allowable only if there is "no significant element of personal pleasure, recreation or vacation" in the away-from-home travel.

The travel-expense disallowance rules apply to payments made directly by the taxpayer of his or her own expenses or of an associated person, such as a member of the taxpayer's family, as well as indirectly through reimbursement by the charity. A reimbursement includes any arrangement for the taxpayer to make a payment to the charity and its payment of the taxpayer's travel outlays. To stop an end run around the disallowance rules, the new law also bars reciprocal arrangements, where two unrelated taxpayers pay each other's expenses or members of a group contribute to a fund that pays for all of their expenses.

Exception. The deduction remains available for payment by the taxpayer of expenses for third parties who are participants in the charitable activity.

Example. Beverly Poppell, a Girl Scout leader, takes her scouts on a camping trip. Beverly gets a deduction for her payment of expenses for girls who belong to the group and are unrelated to her, but not for expenses for her own children.

On the plus side, you do not lose a deduction for your own expenses merely because you enjoy taking care of chores for a charity.

For instance, what about Beverly's own expenses? They are deductible, provided "she is on duty in a genuine and substantial sense throughout the trip, even if she enjoys the trip or supervising children." But her expenses are nondeductible if she (1) "only has nominal duties relating to the performance of services" for the group or (2) "for significant portions of the trip is not required to perform services."

No effect on other deductions. The disallowance rules are inapplicable to deductions (other than for charitable travel) for travel on behalf of a charitable organization. Those rules, for example, do not affect the deductibility of business expenses incurred by an employee of a charity.

CASUALTY LOSS NONDEDUCTIBLE TO EXTENT INSURANCE CLAIM NOT FILED

The law allows an individual to deduct a personal casualty loss only for the portion in excess of 10% of adjusted gross income. Several court cases have held that the loss remains deductible when a person has insurance coverage and chooses not to file a claim with the insurer.

The Tax Reform Act prohibits a deduction to the extent that the loss is covered by insurance and no claim is filed. This change applies to losses sustained after 1986.

CASUALTY LOSS DEDUCTION FOR DEPOSITS LOST IN BANK FAILURES

The law allows individuals to take bad-debt deductions for losses on deposits in financial institutions, such as commercial banks, thrift institutions or insured credit unions. An individual can claim the loss in the year in which it is determined that there is no reasonable prospect of recovery, in the same way as any other bad debt loss. Also, a bad debt loss comes under the rules that limit deductions for short-term capital losses (an offset against any capital gains and $3,000 of other income each year), unless the deposit was made in connection with the individual's trade or business.

The Tax Reform Act retroactively gives individuals another option, starting with returns for 1983. A person can elect to take a casualty loss deduction for a loss on a deposit in a financial institution. The casualty loss (which is deductible only for the portion in excess of 10% of adjusted gross income) can be claimed for the year in which the loss can be reasonably estimated.

The casualty loss election is subject to several restrictions. It is available only where the loss arises as a result of the bankruptcy or insolvency of the financial institution. No election is possible, however, for someone who owns 1% or more of the value of the stock of the financial institution in which the loss was sustained or is an officer of that institution. Nor is there an election for certain persons related to those owners or officers.

A person who elects to treat the loss as a casualty loss cannot claim it as a bad debt deduction. Once the election is made, an individual is limited to a casualty loss deduction for a loss on other deposits in the same institution, unless the IRS authorizes a bad debt deduction.

NOTE: A person does not have to claim the loss for the year in which the loss can first be reasonably estimated. He or she can claim the loss in a later year, either as a casualty loss or as a bad debt.

UNREIMBURSED MOVING EXPENSES BECOME ITEMIZED DEDUCTION

Under the rules for a return for 1986, moving expenses are classified as an "above-the-line" adjustment, that is, a subtraction from gross income to arrive at adjusted gross income that is deductible by individuals, regardless of whether they itemize. Starting with returns for 1987 to be filed in 1988, the Tax Reform Act classifies deductible moving expenses as an itemized deduction, which means they are unavailable to persons who forego itemizing and use the standard deductions.

NOTE: The new itemized deduction for moving expenses is not subject to the 2% floor for most miscellaneous itemized deductions. The new 2% floor is discussed later in this chapter.

Meal expenses during a tax-deductible, work-related move. Prior law allowed a 100% deduction for meals consumed during a work-related move. The Tax Reform Act imposes a new 20% disallowance rule on those meals. See the discussion in chapter 10 of business travel and entertainment expenses.

TRAVEL AS A FORM OF EDUCATION BECOMES NONDEDUCTIBLE

The new law bars any deductions for travel expenditures by teachers and others where their travel is a form of education, starting with returns for 1987 to be filed in 1988. The complete prohibition applies to travel deductions that are otherwise allowable only because the travel itself is educational. But the law retains deductions for travel that is necessary to engage in activities that give rise to deductible education.

Example. Jane Corning is a French teacher who uses a sabbatical leave from her school for a journey to France to improve her understanding of its language and culture. Her travel costs are nondeductible.

Example. Ruth Stone, who is employed by a school to teach courses on French literature, goes to Paris to do specific library research that cannot be done elsewhere, or to take courses available only at the Sorbonne. Assuming her nontravel research or courses are deductible, her travel costs are also deductible.

NOTE: Just because Ruth Stone steers clear of the educational travel prohibition does not mean that she gets to fully deduct her travel expenses. The travel deduction is trimmed by these new limitations:

● Meals must be reduced by 20%. See the discussion in chapter 10 of meal expenses.

● Remaining unreimbursed away-from-home travel expenses are allowable only to the extent they exceed 2% of her adjusted gross income. See the discussion later in this chapter of unreimbursed employee business expenses.

INVESTMENT SEMINARS BECOME NONDEDUCTIBLE

The new law prohibits deductions for costs of attending conventions, seminars or similar meetings for investment purposes, starting with returns for 1987 to be filed in 1988. The disallowance, though, is aimed solely at expenses incurred for investment reasons, as when an investor seeks to obtain information about whether to buy or sell particular stocks, not those incurred for business reasons, as when a financial adviser meets with prospective clients.

Example. International Investors holds a convention at which stock market investors pay for the opportunity to discuss strategies with representatives of brokerage firms and listen to presentations from executives about their companies. *Result:* The new law bars deductions by the investors for their expenses, but does not affect the deductibility of expenses by stock brokers and others at the convention for business reasons.

What expenses are disallowed? Among the expenses disallowed for the investor are: travel to the convention site, attendance fees and meals, lodging and local travel while attending.

MAJOR CHANGES FOR MOST MISCELLANEOUS ITEMIZED DEDUCTIONS AND MOST EMPLOYEE BUSINESS EXPENSES

The Tax Reform Act creates a new category of itemized deductions, starting with returns for 1987 to be filed in 1988. The Act combines most miscellaneous itemized deductions with most employee business expenses (other than expenses that are reimbursed by a person's employer) into one category.

Besides being deductible only if a person itemizes, these expenses are subject to a new floor. They are allowable only to the extent that their total exceeds 2% of a person's adjusted gross income for the year. Anything below the 2% floor is nondeductible.

The 2% floor is subject to a number of exceptions. These exceptions allow an itemizer to continue to deduct the full amount of certain miscellaneous itemized deductions and unreimbursed employee business expenses.

What follows is a detailed look at these sweeping changes.

How the old law worked. Under the rules for a return for 1986, there are two categories of employee business expenses—"above the line" and "below the line." Several types of employee business expenses are classified as above-the-line adjustments. This means that they are subtractions from gross income to arrive at adjusted gross income. Like other adjustments, such as contributions to IRAs and alimony payments, these employee business expenses are deductible by individuals, regardless of whether they itemize their deductions.

Other kinds of employee expenses, as well as other miscellaneous expenses, such as payments to return preparers, are classified as below-the-line adjustments. This means that they are deductible by itemizers, but not by nonitemizers who use the standard deduction.

Above-the-line. In addition to reimbursed employee expenses, this category includes three types of unreimbursed employee business expenses:

● Travel, meals and lodging while away from home;

● Local transportation expenses, such as job-to-job travel, as opposed to commuting; and

● Expenses of outside salespersons (those who solicit business as full-time salespersons for an employer away from their employer's place of business.

Below-the-line. This category of miscellaneous itemized deductions includes these items:

● **Employee business expenses.** These deductibles (other than those in the above the line category) encompass unreimbursed expenses for, among other things, entertainment, subscriptions to business publications, use of home telephone for business, education (to the extent the outlays neither qualify a person for a new job nor enable him to meet the minimum entry-level educational requirements for his present employment), searching for a new job in the same line of work, union and professional association dues, work clothes and uniforms that are required as a condition of employment and not suitable for everyday use, and qualifying home-office costs.

● **Investment expenses.** Among the qualifying outlays are investment counsel and trust administration fees, subscriptions to investment advisory publications, rentals of safe deposit boxes and legal fees incurred in collecting income.

● **Tax-related expenses and other miscellaneous deductions.** This grouping includes things like fees for return preparation or for tax advice in connection with such matters as a divorce, estate planning or the negotiation of an employment contract, as well as appraisals to determine the amount of a casualty loss or charitable contribution of property. It also includes expenses incurred in connection with a hobby (an activity engaged in for recreational reasons, as opposed to a venture undertaken to turn a profit—say, collecting and selling coins and stamps as a hobby), *other* than expenses that generally are deductible without regard to whether the activity is a business engaged in for profit, such as interest, state and local taxes and bad debts.

How the new law works. The new law leaves unchanged above-the-line treatment for (1) all business expenses of sole proprietors and partners; (2) expenses of producing rental or royalty income; and (3) *reimbursed* employee expenses. These three types of expenses remain deductible as subtractions from gross income to arrive at adjusted gross income, whether or not a person itemizes.

NOTE: Congressional committee explanations clarify the treatment of employee-incurred expenses that are reimbursable under an arrangement between the employee and employer, but not fully reimbursed by an employer. The unreimbursed expenses are allowable only as an itemized deduction and subject to the 2% floor.

Expenses that remain deductible without a 2% floor. The new law allows *itemizers* to retain a *full* deduction, *without* a 2% floor, for the following expenses:

● **Impairment-related work expenses of a handicapped person.** These are mainly expenses for attendant care services at the individual's place of employment.

● **Estate tax in the case of income in respect of a decedent.** If you receive income that was earned by, but not paid to a decedent before death, you are said to have "income in respect of a decedent." You report the income, and if an estate has paid a Federal estate tax on the income, you may deduct part of the estate tax allocated to the income.

● **Certain adjustments where a taxpayer restores amounts held under a claim of right.** This deduction comes into play when, for instance, there is a repayment of salary reported in an earlier year.

● **Amortizable bond premium.** This is the extra amount paid for a bond in excess of its face amount.

● **Gambling losses.** The deduction is for losses up to, but not exceeding, gambling income.

● **Expenses of short sales.** These are expenses in the nature of interest.

● **Certain costs of cooperative housing corporations.** These are deductions for mortgage interest and real estate taxes.

● **Certain terminated annuity payments.**

Expenses subject to the 2% floor. The new law allows *itemizers* to deduct expenses in this category only to the extent that their total exceeds 2% of adjusted gross income. Expenses subject to the 2% floor include:

● All prior-law miscellaneous expenses, except for the ones listed above, such as gambling losses, that remain fully deductible.

● All *unreimbursed* employee business expenses deductible under prior law as below-the-line adjustments, such as employment related education costs. Remember, though, that unreimbursed meal and entertainment expenses are subject to the 20% disallowance rule for meals and entertainment (see the discussion in chapter 10) *before* applying the 2% floor.

There is, however, an exception to the 2% floor for certain performing artists. That exception is discussed below.

● All *unreimbursed* employee business expenses deductible under prior law as above-the-line adjustments. That encompasses travel, meals and lodging while away from home, local transportation and expenses of outside salespersons.

Outside salespersons. The preferential treatment they received under prior law is no longer available. Starting in 1987, they are in the same boat as other employees. They must itemize and are subject to the 2% floor.

Interplay of 2% floor and other limitations. Congressional committee reports explain the interplay between the 2% floor and other limitations, such as the new 20% disallowance rules for business meals and entertainment expenses. (Meals and entertainment expenses are discussed in chapter 10.) Taxpayers must apply these other limitations before they apply the 2% floor.

Example. Lois Gaeta has an adjusted gross income of $60,000 and is an outside salesperson for Procrustes Furniture. For simplicity, assume that her only miscellaneous itemized deduction is $2,000 for business meals away from home for which she has not been reimbursed by Procrustes. Lois computes her $400 net miscellaneous itemized deduction as follows:

Unreimbursed meal expenses	$2,000
Less: 20% disallowance	(400)
	$1,600
Less: 2% of adjusted gross income	1,200
Net miscellaneous itemized deduction	$ 400

Special break for qualifying performing artists. Starting with returns for 1987, certain performing artists may be able to report their income and expenses as if they were independent contractors. Unlike other employees, their expenses are not subject to the 2% floor.

This break provides only limited relief. It is available solely to performers who are able to pass a three-step test. First, the performer works for at least two employers in the performing arts during the year. Second, performing artist expenses exceed 10% of his or her wages from performing. Third, adjusted gross income (before subtracting performing artist expenses) is not more than $16,000.

RESTRICTIONS ON HOME-OFFICE DEDUCTIONS

The new law imposes several limitations on deductions for business use of a home, starting with returns for 1987 to be filed in 1988.

Rental to employer does not avoid restrictions on home-office deductions. The restrictions on deductions for home-office business expenses (other than expenses allowable in the absence of business use, such as home mortgage interest and real property taxes) can no longer be side-stepped by an arrangement under which an employee rents a portion of his or her home to an employer. This denial of deductions for a lease by an employee to an employer also applies to a lease by an individual who is an independent contractor to a party for whom the individual performs services.

Why the change? To close a rental loophole opened by a Tax Court decision. The Tax Court allowed a rental-expense deduction claimed by the managing director of an accounting firm for the lease to his firm of a room in his home where he met with other directors. He took advantage of an exception that excuses someone who rents out part of his home from the strict general-business use requirements (regular and exclusive use either as a principal place of business or to meet patients, clients or customers and, in the case of an employee, for the convenience of the employer) that must be met before qualifying for a home-office deduction.

NOTE: The law cautions that withholding and employment tax requirements cannot be sidestepped by an employer merely by an agreement with an employee that payments that are actually wages are to be called "rent" under a "rental" or "lease" agreement.

Deductions limited to net income from business. Prior law limited home-office deductions to the gross income from the business, with no carryover for costs in excess of the limit. The new law places a limit on home-office deductions *related* to use of the office itself, such as rent, depreciation, utilities and insurance, other than expenses that are deductible in any event, such as home mortgage interest and real estate taxes. The limit is the difference between (1) gross income from the business and (2) all deductible expenses that are *not related* to use of the office itself, such as supplies, secretaries and postage. Translation: No current deduction for rent or other home-office expenses to the extent they create or increase a net loss from the business.

All is not necessarily lost for deductions disallowed solely because of the gross-income limitation. These deductions can be carried forward to offset net income from the business in subsequent years. Expenses carried forward, however, are subject to the continuing application of the income limitation to prevent the use of such deductions to create or increase a net loss in any year from the business activity.

Example. A business run out of a home has gross income of $35,000; it incurs rent and utility expenses of $5,000, while supplies and other expenses aggregate $33,000. The rental deduction is limited to $2,000, with a carryforward of $3,000.

HOBBY LOSS RULES TIGHTENED

There is a one-way tax rule for hobbies: Income from a hobby is taxable; losses are not deductible. The losses are considered nondeductible personal losses. The question of whether an activity, such as dog breeding or collecting and selling stamps and coins, is a hobby or sideline business arises when losses are incurred. You may be able to resolve this question in your favor by taking advantage of a "presumption." There is a presumption, which can be rebutted by the IRS, that you are in an activity for profit, rather than a hobby, if it is profitable in three out of five consecutive years (two out of seven years in the case of horse breeding, training, racing or showing). The Tax Reform Act tightened the presumption rule from two-out-of-five to three-out-of-five for taxable years beginning after 1986, but left unchanged the two-out-of-seven rule for horse breeding, etc.

REPEAL OF DEDUCTION FOR WORKING COUPLES

The Tax Reform Act repeals the deduction for a two-earner married couple filing jointly, starting with returns for 1987 to be filed in 1988. On returns for 1986 and earlier years, a couple can deduct 10% of the earnings of the lower-paid spouse, up to a maximum of $3,000.

TAX CREDIT FOR POLITICAL CONTRIBUTIONS REPEALED

The new law repeals the credit, starting with returns for 1987 to be filed in 1988. On returns for 1986 and earlier years, individuals are allowed a credit of up to $50 ($100 on a joint return) for half of their contributions to political candidates and certain political campaign organizations.

HOUSING ALLOWANCES FOR MINISTERS AND MILITARY PERSONNEL

The new law authorizes preferential treatment for tax-free parsonage housing allowances received by ministers or off-base housing allowances received by military personnel. Ministers and military personnel are entitled to deduct all payments for mortgage interest and property taxes on their homes. They do not have to reduce their deductions for interest and taxes to the extent these expenses are allocable to the tax-free allowances.

This rule change applies retroactively. However, taxpayers cannot reopen any taxable years closed by the statute of limitations to claim refunds based on the change.

ALIMONY RULES REVISED

For decrees issued and agreements made after December 31, 1986, the new law makes these changes: (1) An agreement does not have to state that there is no liability to make payments after death and (2) the recapture period is reduced from six to three years with a new $15,000-payment test. Recapture does not apply to temporary support payments or to fluctuating payments based on salary, business or investment income.

4

MORE KINDS OF INCOME BECOME REPORTABLE

RESTRICTIONS ON TAX-FREE TREATMENT OF SCHOLARSHIPS AND FELLOWSHIPS

The new law overhauls the rules authorizing tax-free treatment for individuals who receive scholarships and fellowship grants from colleges, universities and other educational institutions. These wide-ranging revisions include a limitation of the exclusion, that is, tax-free treatment for degree candidates and a repeal of the exclusion for nondegree candidates. The revised rules apply to scholarships and fellowships granted after August 16, 1986, starting with returns for 1987 to be filed in 1988.

Degree candidates. Prior law excluded from taxable income scholarships and fellowship grants received from schools by degree candidates for their tuition, matriculation and other fees and regular living expenses, like room and board. The exclusion for students seeking sheepskins also applied to allowances received to cover their expenses for travel, research, clerical help or equipment.

The new law allows a taxable-income exclusion only for the amount of a grant that Joe or Josephine College actually uses to cover these items: (1) Tuition and fees for enrollment or attendance; and (2) fees, books, supplies and equipment required for courses at an educational institution. No longer does a student enjoy tax freedom for grant dollars that pay for room and board or that cover expenses for travel, research, clerical help or equipment.

No tracing-of-funds requirement. Congressional committee reports remind the IRS that the new limitations should not add to the paperwork burden for degree candidates. They do not have to track their spending of grant dollars to establish their eligibility for tax-free treatment of those funds.

Example. The tab for tuition and equipment is $10,000 at Thurber University. It awards a $10,000 science scholarship to Jack Smurch. Jack is relived of taxes on his scholarship without having to trace specific dollars to specific outlays. He need not show how much he pays for each chemistry, physics and biology course and for beakers, bottles and other equipment for each course, provided Thurber requires him to use the $10,000 for courses and equipment. No exclusion is allowed, though, for anything above $10,000 received by Jack, even though Thurber calls the excess a scholarship grant. Nor is the scholarship winner entitled to exclude any part of the $10,000 that is designated or earmarked for room and board or other, impermissible purposes at the university.

Payments for teaching or research. Ordinarily, the IRS collects its share of payments that are compensation for services. But prior law made a special exception for a student who received part of a scholarship or fellowship grant as payment for teaching, research or other part-time services. The student sidestepped taxes on those chores when they were required of all candidates for the particular degree.

The new law says a person must treat this type of compensation as taxable income when the payments are for services required as a condition for receiving a scholarship or a tuition reduction. This holds true, say Congressional committee reports, whether the compensation takes the form of a paycheck, which the student then uses for tuition, or, in lieu of a paycheck, the school reduces its tuition charge for a student who is its employee.

Nondegree candidates. The new law scraps tax-free treatment for grant funds received by students who take courses but are not pursuing a degree. Prior law capped at $10,800 the amount of grant dollars that eluded taxes, but left uncapped the exclusion for the part of a grant received by a nondegree candidate to cover expenses for travel, research, clerical help or equipment. The new law taxes the recipient of any grant, for whatever purpose.

Other escape hatches remain open. The repeal of this exclusion does not affect the applicability of an exclusion under a different rule for employer-provided educational assistance to an employee who is a nondegree candidate. (The educational assistance exclusion is discussed in chapter 9.) Nor does the repeal affect the write-off by a nondegree candidate of unreimbursed educational outlays as business expenses.

NOTE: The full deduction may not be available to a nondegree candidate who is an employee and must claim the unreimbursed educational expenses as a miscellaneous itemized deduction. The Tax Reform Act places a nondeductible 2%-of-adjusted-gross-income "floor" under certain miscellaneous itemized deductions, including educational expenses. See the discussion of miscellaneous deductions in chapter 3.

Federal grants. The new law repeals the exclusion for certain Federal grants where the recipient is required to perform future services as a Federal employee.

TAX-FREE TREATMENT OF UNEMPLOYMENT COMPENSATION ENDED

Under the new law, there is no longer a partial exclusion, that is, exemption from taxes, for unemployment compensation benefits. All benefits are included in income, starting with returns for 1987 to be filed in 1988.

TIGHTER RESTRICTIONS ON AWARDS FOR ARTISTIC AND SIMILAR ACHIEVEMENTS

The new law limits the availability of tax-free treatment for prizes and awards made primarily in recognition of religious, charitable, scientific, educational, artistic, literary or civic achievements. Under the rules for returns for 1986 and earlier years, tax-free treatment is available only if the winner satisfied two requirements. First, the recipient is selected without action on his or her part, that is, he or she did not specifically apply for the prize or award by, say, entering a contest. Second, the recipient is not required, as a condition of receipt, to render substantial future services.

The new law retains the two requirements and adds a third. It allows an exclusion from income, that is, tax-free treatment, only if the winner assigns the award to charity, starting with returns for 1987 to be filed in 1988. Specifically, the recipient must "designate" that the prize or award is to be transferred by the payor to a governmental unit or a tax-exempt charitable, educational, or religious organization, contributions to which are deductible.

No double break. Does a winner who passes the three-step test for exclusion of the award also get a charitable deduction for assignment of the award to, among others, his Uncle Sam or his alma mater? The answer is that there is no deduction break for the winner or for the organization that pays the award.

The tax-right way to designate. Congressional committee reports set an exclusion-qualification deadline that bars the winner's use of the award proceeds before they are assigned to charity. To pass muster, the winner's designation and the award-paying organization's fulfillment of that designation must occur before any impermissible use by the winner of the money or other property awarded. Otherwise, no exclusion is allowed and the award is taxable.

In the case of a cash award, the designation/ fulfillment has to occur before the winner spends, deposits or otherwise invests the funds. Other impermissible uses include use of the property with the winner's permission or by someone associated with the winner, such as a family member.

INTEREST ON INSTALLMENT PAYMENTS OF LIFE INSURANCE PROCEEDS

Generally, life insurance proceeds received because of the death of the insured are tax free, while interest paid on proceeds left with the insurer is taxable. Under prior law, however, a surviving spouse who elected to receive installments, rather than a lump sum, did not pay tax on the first $1,000 of interest received each year.

The new law repeals the $1,000 annual exclusion. This repeal applies to amounts received with respect to deaths that occur after the date on which President Reagan signed the Tax Reform Act.

REDUCTION OR DISALLOWANCE OF FOREIGN EARNED INCOME EXCLUSION

The law authorizes an exclusion, that is, tax-free treatment, up to a specified amount for income earned by U.S. citizens and residents who work abroad (other than as U.S. government employees). To qualify for the exclusion, they must pass a foreign residence or physical presence test.

The Tax Reform Act of 1986 reduces the maximum annual exclusion from $80,000 to $70,000, starting with returns for 1987 to be filed in 1988. Before the new Act, the exclusion had been scheduled to increase to $85,000 for 1988, $90,000 for 1989 and $95,000 for 1990.

Also, the new law bars an exclusion for Americans in foreign countries, such as Cuba and Libya, to which travel is generally prohibited. This limitation applies starting with returns for 1987.

TAXATION OF U.S. GOVERNMENT EMPLOYEES IN PANAMA

The new law specifies that the Panama Canal treaty does not authorize an exemption from U.S. taxes for U.S. employees of the Panama Canal Commission. Also, employees of the Panama Canal Commission and the Defense Department are entitled to certain tax-free allowances like those available for employees of the State Department stationed in Panama. These changes apply starting with returns for 1987 to be filed in 1988.

RULES FOR FOSTER CARE PAYMENTS LIBERALIZED

The law authorizes an exclusion, that is, tax-free treatment, for a foster parent who receives reimbursements from a governmental agency for the cost of caring for a foster child in the home of the foster parent. Under the prior rules, the exclusion was available only if the foster parent accounted for the expenses.

The Tax Reform Act makes two changes in the rules. First, the exclusion also applies to payments reserved for the cost of caring for a foster adult. Second, the Act eliminates the accounting requirement. From now on, the exclusion applies to all amounts received by a foster parent for care of a foster child, not just reimbursements.

These changes apply starting with returns for 1986 to be filed in 1987.

5

FAMILY INCOME PLANNING

TAXING CHILDREN'S INCOME

The easiest way for higher-bracket parents to shift income from themselves to their lower-bracket children is to make gifts to them of money or other income-producing assets. As a general rule, the Tax Reform Act stops parental income shifting to children under the age of 14, starting with returns for 1987 to be filed in 1988.

The Act does so by generally taxing investment earnings above $1,000 for a child under age 14 at the parents' top tax rate. It makes no difference whether the investment income comes from money or other assets given to the child by a parent or by someone other than a parent—for instance, a grandparent. Nor does it matter that such gifts were made before 1987. If the child is 14 or over, income continues to be taxed at the child's rate.

An under-14 child's investment earnings below $1,000 are taxed under another new set of rules. The child can use up to $500 of his or her standard deduction ($2,540 for 1987; see chapter 2) to offset investment earnings. The next $500 is taxed at the child's rate. What these complicated rules work out to is that the parents' rate usually applies only to earnings above $1,000.

What the old rules allowed. Under prior law, a family was able to reduce its aggregate tax liability by shifting income-producing property among family members. Consider, for example, parents who wanted to minimize taxes paid on income from funds set aside for the college education of their child. A common maneuver for these parents, whose dividend income would otherwise be taxed at their high tax bracket, was to transfer shares of stock into a custodian account for their child. By doing so, they deflected part of the family's income to a child taxed at a lower rate.

What the new rules allow. There are two sets of rules for taxing what the law refers to as unearned income, that is, investment earnings received by children. The first set is for children under 14 years of age, while the second is for children 14 or over.

Children under the age of 14. In the case of an under-14 child, investment earnings of more than $1,000 usually are taxed at the parent's top rate, that is, as if the parent had received the income, rather than the child's lower rate. The under-14 rules remain applicable until the child reaches age 14.

Exemption from the under-14 rules. Certain kinds of income are exempt from the new rules and continue to be taxed at the child's rate. The exemption is for (1) investment earnings below $1,000, as a general rule, and (2) all wages earned by the child, whether the wages come from babysitting, delivering newspapers or even from a job with a business owned by a parent.

Children over the age of 14. The under-14 rules cease to be applicable when a child attains the age of 14 before the close of the taxable year in question. Instead, a more advantageous set of rules applies. In general, all investment earnings, whether they are received from a parental or nonparental source, are taxed at the child's rate, as are wages.

Trust income. Special rules apply to income received by children from property put into temporary trust arrangements (known as Clifford or ten-year trusts). These trusts are discussed in the next section of this chapter. When the income received by an under-14 child is from property that a parent put into a trust before March 2, 1986, the income can be taxed as if received by the *parent.* Such income continues to be taxed at the *child's* rate when the child is over 14. In the case of trust transfers after March 1, 1986, all of the trust income received by the child is taxed as if received by the parent or other grantor who sets up the trust.

RESTRICTIONS ON USING TRUSTS TO SHIFT INCOME TO CHILDREN

The previous section explains new limitations on shifting of income by parent-to-child asset transfers. There are also new restrictions on the use of trusts to accomplish income shifts.

What the old rules allowed. By way of background, what are known as the grantor trust rules treat the grantor of a trust as its owner when there is a transfer of property to a trust by a grantor who retains certain powers or interests over the trust. As a result, income attributable to the trust is taxed to its grantor, that is, the person who sets up the trust, rather than to its beneficiary.

But a prior-law exception to the grantor trust rules allowed a grantor-to-beneficiary shift of the taxes on trust income used to pay for, say, college costs. The exception became applicable when at least ten years had to elapse before certain powers and interests that were retained by the grantor could revert to the grantor.

Consequently, a long-favored way for many high bracket individuals to shift income from themselves to children, grandchildren and other lower-taxed family members is to transfer money, stocks, real estate or other income-generating assets for a period of at least ten years into reversionary trust arrangements known as "Clifford" or "short-term" trusts. During the period that the temporary trust is in existence, the income is taxed to the child or other person named to receive the trust income. At the end of the trust period, the grantor regains the trust corpus, which is legalese for the assets used to fund the Clifford Trust.

A spousal remainder trust provides another way for a parent-to-child shift of the taxes on income earmarked for educational expenses. One parent funds the trust. It can be set up for less than ten years and the specified period can end upon the child's completion of college, with the trust assets then becoming the property of the grantor's spouse.

What the new rules allow. The 1986 Tax Reform Act abolishes income-shifting breaks for Clifford Trusts. As a general rule, income from ten-year and other grantor trusts is taxed to the grantor, not the beneficiary, if the property put in the trust will revert to the grantor or the grantor's spouse. It is immaterial how long the trust lasts.

The ten-year rule was replaced with a rule that treats a trust as a grantor trust where the grantor has a reversionary interest whose value, at the time of the transfer of the property into the trust, amounts to more than 5% of the value of the transferred property.

Also, if a grantor's spouse is living with the grantor at the time of the creation of any power or interest held by the spouse, the grantor is treated as holding that power or interest—a restriction that kills spousal remainder trusts.

When the new rules take effect. Generally, the revised rules apply to trust transfers made after March 1, 1986. That translates into no income shifting for income from Clifford Trusts started after that date.

There is, however, an exception from the new rules for Clifford Trusts that were created and funded before March 2, 1986. Such trusts are unaffected by the new rules and can continue to shift income to the beneficiary.

Remember, though, that the income shifted through pre-March 2 trusts is subject to the new rules for taxing investment earnings received by children under the age of 14. Those rules are discussed in the previous section of this chapter.

To illustrate, assume that a parent set up and funded a pre-March 2 trust. The trust named an under-14 child as beneficiary. *Result*: The trust income can be taxed at the parent's tax rate, not the child's.

Assume, instead, that the child is over 14. In that event, the trust income continues to be taxed at the child's rate.

INCOME TAX RATES FOR TRUSTS AND ESTATES

Trusts and estates are taxed on their retained income. The new law revises the tax rate schedules for retained income. These changes apply to taxable years of both new and existing nongrantor trusts (but not grantor trusts, such as ten-year trust or spousal remainder trusts) and estates beginning after 1986.

For 1987, the rates start at 11% on the first $500 of taxable income of nongrantor trusts and go as high as 38.5% on taxable income in excess of $15,150. For 1988 and subsequent years the tax is 15% on the first $5,000 of taxable income of nongrantor trusts and 28% on trust taxable income in excess of $5,000. There is a phase-out of the 15% bracket for trust taxable income between $13,000 and $26,000.

The tax rate for estates under the new law is the same as that for nongrantor trusts.

TAXABLE YEARS OF TRUSTS

The new law requires all trusts, whether existing or newly created, to use a calendar year as their taxable year. There is an exception for certain tax-exempt and charitable trusts. They can continue to use a fiscal year.

What is the reason for the change? It is to end a break available under prior law when a trust has a taxable year that is different than the taxable year of its beneficiaries. Prior law allowed the deferral of taxation by one month for each month that the taxable year of the trust ended sooner than the taxable year of its beneficiaries. Take, for example, a trust with a taxable year ending on January 31 and with the trust beneficiary on a calendar year. The taxation of trust income that was distributed to the beneficiary was deferred 11 months.

When the revised rules take effect. They apply to taxable years beginning after 1986. There are, however, special transition provisions for existing trusts.

For example, a trust with a taxable year that ends on January 31 must adopt a taxable year that ends on December 31, 1987. For 1987, the trust will have a short taxable year, that is, a taxable year of less than 12 months.

A relief provision alleviates the bunching of income in 1987 that arises from the change in taxable years. The taxable income to the beneficiary that is attributable to any short taxable year for 1987 required under the new law can be reported in equal amounts over a four-year period that begins with the year of change.

To illustrate, assume a trust has a taxable year that ends on January 31. It adopts a taxable year that ends on December 31, which results in a short taxable year for 1987. The amount includible in the income of the beneficiary for the short year is $4,000. With that set of figures, the beneficiary includes $1,000 in income on his or her return for 1987, 1988, 1989 and 1990.

CHARITABLE DONATIONS OF CONSERVATION EASEMENTS

The new law allows gift and estate tax deductions for certain irrevocable charitable donations in perpetuity of real property easements to charitable organizations, to the United States, or to a State or local government. It is immaterial that the contributions fail to meet the requirement for deductibility for income tax purposes that the contributions be for conservation purposes. This rule applies to transfers and contributions after 1986.

STOCK SOLD TO ESOPs

Under the new law, there is an exemption from estate taxes for 50% of the proceeds realized on the sale by an executor of stock in the estate to an employee stock ownership plan. This rule applies to sales after the date President Reagan signed the 1986 Tax Reform Act and before January 1, 1992, by an estate required to file a return (including extensions of time to file) after the signing date.

6
INVESTMENT DECISIONS

NEW RULES FOR CAPITAL GAINS

The Tax Reform Act eliminates special tax treatment for income from long-term capital gains, a preference that has been part of the Internal Revenue Code since 1921. The Act accomplishes this by doing away with the exclusion from income for 60% of gains on assets owned longer than six months, starting with returns for 1987 to be filed in 1988.

Under the rules for a return for 1986, the top tax rate on long-term capital gains is 20%. The new rules tax long-term capital gains at the same rate as ordinary income, subject to a top rate of 28%. This holds true even though the top rate for 1987 is 38.5% (see the discussion of tax rates in chapter 2).

Short-term capital gains. They are taxed like ordinary income. Consequently, their top rate is 50% for 1986, 38.5% for 1987 and 28% after 1987.

NOTE: The Tax Reform Act does not do away with the distinction between capital gains and losses and ordinary income and deductions. For example, as under current law, you still net your capital gains and losses. Capital losses fully offset capital gains. However, to the extent your capital losses exceed your capital gains, the net loss can be deducted against no more than $3,000 of ordinary income in any one year. One difference from prior law: Starting in 1987, both long- and short-term capital losses offset ordinary income on a dollar-for-dollar basis. Under prior law, one dollar of long-term capital loss could offset no more than 50¢ of ordinary income. Capital losses that cannot offset the current year's ordinary income can still be carried forward to later years.

Tax strategy. The new law makes 1986 the last year for a tax choice on gains from sales of stocks during the last five trading days in December. You can treat a gain as an installment sale and pay tax in 1987 (when the cash settlement is made). Or you can elect out of installment tax treatment and pay tax in 1986 (the year you made the sale).

The tax flexibility you have by selling listed stocks or bonds during the last five trading days is especially important in 1986. You can have net short-term gain taxed in 1987 under the installment sale rules. Or you can have net long-term gain taxed in 1986 by electing out of installment sale treatment.

The Tax Reform Act takes away the choice of when to pay tax on sales of publicly traded property in the last five trading days. Starting in 1987, you must pay tax in the year you receive payment for the stock (see chapter 12).

DIVIDEND EXCLUSION FOR INDIVIDUALS REPEALED

The new law ends the exclusion for qualifying dividends of up to $100 for single returns and $200 for joint returns, starting with returns for 1987 to be filed in 1988.

RULES EASED FOR INCENTIVE STOCK OPTIONS

Many corporations include stock options in their compensation package to attract and motivate executives. The options provide key employees with an opportunity to buy company stock at a bargain price.

There are two basic kinds of executive option plans—statutory (that is, incentive stock options) and nonstatutory (that is, nonqualified).

There are important tax differences. With incentive stock options no tax is owed until the stock acquired with the option is sold. Tax is owed when a nonqualified option is exercised.

The employer also gets a deduction when the nonqualified option is exercised. The employer with the incentive stock option gets no deduction.

These important tax differences remain in the wake of the Tax Reform Act. However, because of the new legislation, there are new similarities:

Sequence of exercise. Starting with options issued after 1986, an executive no longer must exercise incentive stock options in the order they are granted to him or her. This is the same rule that has applied to nonqualified options. What this means: If the price of the stock falls well below the option price, the executive can be issued a second incentive option with a lower exercise price.

No capital gain. Under prior law, with an incentive stock option, the bargain element (the spread between the option's exercise price and the price of the stock) was taxed as long-term capital gain when the stock was sold (as long as the stock was held for more than one year before sale). With the loss of the capital gain exclusion, the bargain element in both options is taxed at the same rates as ordinary income.

Special break. For 1987 only, capital gain will continue to have an edge over ordinary income. The top tax on capital gain will be 28%; the top tax on ordinary income will be 38.5% (see chapter 2). So incentive stock sold during 1987 will be more favorably taxed than nonqualified stock sold during the year (assuming a one year holding period is met).

New flexibility after 1987. Under prior law, the holder of an incentive stock option forfeited capital gain if he or she sold stock bought with the option, within two years after the option was granted or one year after the stock was bought. Again, with the loss of the tax-favored treatment for capital gains after 1987, the employee can sell the stock immediately after buying it.

Modified dollar caps. There is a limit of $100,000 per employee on incentive stock option grants. Starting in 1987, it applies to the value of stock covered by options that are exercisable in any one calendar year, instead of the value of options granted in any one year.

NOTE: Incentive stock options continue to be subject to the alternative minimum tax for individuals, which is discussed in chapter 2.

TAX STRADDLES

Straddle positions are taken by investors to create a desired tax position without suffering any substantial economic risk. A common straddle position may be taken to claim a loss in one year and a gain in another year or to convert ordinary income into capital gain. The risk of economic loss is eliminated by investing in two similar postions that are affected directly by the same economic movements.

Year-end rule for qualified covered calls. Under prior law, a loss-deferral rule applies to a straddle consisting of stock offset by an option. The rule, however, is subject to an exception for what the law refers to as a qualified covered call option (an option that a stockholder, who is not a dealer, grants on stock traded on a national securities exchange). No exception is available, however, for a taxpayer who fails to hold stock for 30 days after the related call option is disposed of at a loss, where gain on sale of the stock is included in the subsequent year.

The new law revises this rule. The exception is inapplicable and the loss-deferral rule applies when it is the stock that is sold at a loss and the related option that is not held for 30 days thereafter and the gain on it is included in the subsequent year.

TAX-EXEMPT BONDS

The Tax Reform Act leaves unchanged the basic exemption from Federal taxes for bonds issued by state and local governments to finance traditional operations. The Act does impose new restrictions on private use bonds. These are obligations issued to finance activities other than general governmental operations or governmentally owned and operated facilities. There is also a new volume cap on the amount of bonds that a state can issue.

The expanded list of preference items for individuals and corporations that is subject to the alternative minimum tax includes tax-exempt interest on most municipal bonds issued for nonessential functions after August 7, 1986. The alternative minimum tax for individuals is discussed in chapter 2; for corporations, it is discussed in chapter 11.

7
TAX SHELTERS

CRACKDOWN ON TAX SHELTER LOSSES

The 1986 Tax Reform Act attacks tax shelters in several ways. The assault includes strict limitations on deductions for losses from investments in shelters. The tough new rules are aimed mainly at executives, professionals and other prosperous individuals who invest in real estate projects and other transactions that usually generate losses, at least in the short term, and use their losses to offset income that they receive from salaries, investments and other sources.

The 1986 Act targets investors in limited partnerships and other shelters that the new rules define as "passive activities," in which they do not "materially participate," that is, the investors are not regularly, continuously and substantially involved on a day-to-day basis.

NOTE: A wide-ranging attack on all sorts of ventures traditionally thought of as shelters also affects many persons who are unlikely to think of their existing or contemplated business investments as subject to the new rules for shelters—for instance, parents who invest (as opposed to merely lending) in a business run by their child, but do not participate at all in its operations, to cite a common situation.

What the new rules accomplish when you have a loss from a passive activity in which you do not materially participate is to prevent you from using a passive-activity loss to shelter your "active income" from sources such as salaries and other earnings. Nor are you entitled to use that loss to offset "portfolio income," such as dividends, interest and capital gains. You are allowed to write off a loss from one shelter only against income from limited partnerships and other shelters.

What relief becomes available when your loss exceeds income from other shelters for the year in question? You can carry forward this loss, known under the new rules as a suspended loss, to a later year to erase the taxes on income received from other shelters. Suppose, though, that you have yet to use up the suspended loss by the time you decide to sell or otherwise dispose of your investment. In that event, you offset the loss against your otherwise taxable gain on the sale.

Exceptions. These tough curbs on shelter losses are subject to exceptions for three kinds of shelters—(1) rental real estate; (2) tax credits for rehabilitating certain types of buildings and constructing and rehabilitating low-income housing; and (3) working interests in oil and gas drilling operations. Losses or credits from these shelters can be used, within limits, to offset income from all sources, including salaries and portfolio income.

Rental real estate. As a general rule, the new law categorizes the ownership of rental property as a passive activity, regardless of whether the owner materially participates. There is, however, a special provision that authorizes an exception for individuals (but not corporations) who actively manage their rental real estate.

Under this exception, all but the wealthiest landlords can continue to offset the first $25,000 of loss each year from rental real estate against income from any source. To qualify for this break, an individual has to "actively participate" in the management and operation of the property, which is a less stringent standard that the material participation requirement, and have an annual adjusted gross income of under $100,000.

The offset of as much as $25,000 ($12,500 is the ceiling for married persons who file separate returns) begins to phase out for landlords with adjusted gross incomes above $100,000 (without any reduction for passive-activity losses). The maximum offset shrinks by fifty cents for each dollar of income beyond $100,000 and vanishes completely when income surpasses $150,000. *Result*: Persons with incomes above $150,000 are unable to use rental losses to offset income from sources other than shelters.

Unlike the material-participation requirements for most shelters, the active-participation requirement for rental real estate can be satisfied without regular, continuous and substantial involvement in operations by an investor. It is met, according to Congressional committee reports, even if a landlord hires a managing agent to run the property. All that is necessary to pass muster is that the investor help make decisions on such things as tenant selection, rental terms, and repairs and capital expenditures; it's permissible to leave day-to-day operations up to the agent.

Some other fine print worth noting is that the break is available only for an investor who owns at least a 10% interest in the property. But this, of course, includes the typical individual who invests in one- or two-family homes and other small properties.

Example. You own a small apartment building or a beach cottage that you use as a part-time vacation home and retain an agent to run it. You can use up to $25,000 of tax loss from the property to shelter other taxable income, assuming your adjusted gross income is under $100,000.

Credits for rehabilitating certain types of buildings and constructing and rehabilitating low-income housing. These credits can be used to offset up to $25,000 of income from any source. The offset of as much as $25,000 ($12,500 for marrieds filing separately) begins to phase out for individuals with adjusted gross incomes above $200,000 (without any reduction for passive-activity losses). The maximum offset shrinks by fifty cents for each dollar of income beyond $200,000 and vanishes completely when income surpasses $250,000.

In general, the credits for low-income housing apply only to property placed in service before 1991, provided at least 10% of the total low-income housing costs are incurred before 1989.

Working interests in oil and gas drilling operations. These interests are completely exempt from the material-participation requirements for other shelters. Losses from oil and gas working interests remain fully deductible against any kind of income. It makes no difference that the investors are unable to show that they regularly participate in the drilling activity.

Be aware, however, that a "working interest" generally means a higher degree of personal liability than is usually found in the typical oil or gas limited partnership.

For instance, assume that there is an explosion at the drilling site. A "working interest" might require you to lay out more cash, over and above the amount that you originally invested.

When the new rules apply. As a general rule, the new restrictions apply to all shelter losses for taxable years beginning after 1986. It is immaterial that a taxpayer entered into the shelters before 1987.

To cushion the immediate impact of the new rules, there is generally a five-year phase-in of the restrictions for shelters held by taxpayers from the date that President Reagan signed the new law. For shelters acquired before the changes became law, investors can continue to use 65% of the losses to offset all other kinds of income in 1987, which means investors cannot use 35% of their losses. Investors are able to use only 40% of their losses in 1988, 20% in 1989 and 10% in 1990. Starting in 1991, the restrictions apply to all shelter losses.

A closer look. What follows is a more detailed explanation of the new rules.

Losses from passive activities. In general, losses and credits from activities categorized as passive can offset only income from passive activities. Passive-activity losses cannot offset portfolio income, such as interest, dividends, royalties and gains from sales of portfolio property. Nor can they offset income categorized as "positive," such as salaries and commissions. Similarly, passive-activity tax credits (other than foreign tax credits) can offset only the tax payable on passive activity income.

There is a relief for what the law refers to as suspended losses and credits, that is, passive losses in excess of passive income, and excess credits. They may be carried forward and used to offset future years' passive income or, in the case of credits, the tax on that income. Suspended losses become allowable in full when a taxpayer disposes of his or her entire interest in the passive activity.

Who comes under the passive-loss rules? In general, they apply to individuals, estates, trusts, personal service corporations (professional corporations formed by doctors, lawyers and the like), and C corporations (those that are taxed at the corporate level, as opposed to S corporations that are taxed at the shareholder level) that are closely held. C corporations are considered closely held when five or fewer individuals own, directly or indirectly, more than 50% of the stock. It's not just tax shelters that are hit. The wide-ranging rules affect passive interests in any trade or business.

There is a blanket exception from the passive-loss rules for working interests in oil and gas properties and a limited exception for active real estate investors.

There are two categories of passive activities:

(1) Any trade or business, or (to the extent spelled out in IRS administrative regulations) activity conducted for profit in which the taxpayer does not materially participate; and

(2) Any rental activity, whether or not the taxpayer materially participates.

Passive trade or business activities. Any trade or business is a passive activity with respect to a taxpayer who does not materially participate in the enterprise. Material participation is defined as a year-round active involvement in the operations of the activity on a regular, continuous and substantial basis.

Example. Mother supplies Daughter with capital to start a business and become a general partner in the venture. Although Mother approves major capital outlays, she does not participate in the business on a regular basis. *Result*: Mother cannot shelter portfolio or salary income with her share of losses from the business.

What constitutes material participation. According to Congressional committee reports, there are three main factors to be considered. None of them, however, conclusively determines the presence or absence of material participation.

• Is the activity the taxpayer's principal trade or business?

Examples. A person whose main business is farming is more likely to materially participate in a farm than an executive who invests in a farming operation. On the other hand, someone whose sideline business is producing documentaries is not engaged in a passive activity merely because his or her principal business is that of film executive.

● How close is the taxpayer to the activity? An individual is more likely to be actively involved in a business that is located in his or her vicinity. Nevertheless, proximity is not enough. That person still must actively participate in the business. But distance from the enterprise is not always a bar. For example, a software developer who lives in New York may be actively involved in his company, even if its location is California.

● Does the taxpayer have knowledge and experience in the enterprise? For example, a dentist who knows little about cattle is unlikely to be materially involved in a cattle-feeding operation. It makes no difference that the dentist had experience with cattle feeding. The dentist still must be involved in day-to-day operations to steer clear of the passive-loss rules. Put another way, rubber-stamping decisions made by others is insufficient.

There is a special exception for a farmer who materially participates in his or her farm. The farmer retains that status after retirement, as does the spouse of a deceased farmer.

The material-participation rule applies whether a taxpayer (or his or her spouse) owns an interest as a proprietor, general partner, or S corporation shareholder. For a personal service corporation or a closely held C corporation to meet the test, one or more shareholders who own 50% or more of the stock must materially participate in the activity.

There is an alternative test for a closely held C corporation. It can meet the material participation rule if (1) at least one full time employee works full time and year-round in the active management of the activity; (2) at least three employees, other than owners, work full time in the activity for the entire year; and (3) business deductions of the activity exceed 15% of its gross income.

A taxpayer who directly or indirectly owns an interest in any activity as a limited partner automatically fails the material participation test. Congress has authorized the IRS to issue administrative regulations that will prevent taxpayers from manipulating this rule in order to circumvent the passive loss limitation.

Example. A taxpayer would not be able to sop up large passive losses merely by converting his ownership of income-generating activities into limited partnership form. Moreover, income from personal services to the passive activity is not "passive activity income" that can sop up losses from passive activities.

Rental activities. These activities are presumed to be passive and include all activities that generate income from payments for the use of tangible property, rather than for the performance of substantial services. Signposts of a rental activity: a lease term that is long in relation to the property's useful life; day-to-day expenses are insignificant in relation to rents or in relation to depreciation and carrying costs; and no significant services are supplied to each new lessee.

For loss-limitation purposes, rental activities include long-term rentals of apartments, office equipment and automobiles or the rental of a vessel under a bare-boat charter or a plane under a dry lease (no pilot or captain and no fuel), and net-leased property. A property is net-leased if the lessor's deductions (other than rents and reimbursed amounts) are less than 15% of rental income, or where the lessor is guaranteed a specific return or is guaranteed against loss of income. Rental activities do not include short-term car rentals, and rentals of hotel rooms or similar space to transients.

As a general rule, real estate rentals, whether short- or long-term, are presumed to be rental activities. Thus, they are automatically passive in nature.

There are three exceptions. First, real estate dealers are generally not treated as engaging in a passive activity. Second, taxpayers may use up to $25,000 of real estate losses and credit equivalents to shelter non-passive income if they are "active participants," as explained in more detail below. Third, mortgage interest on a principal, that is, year-round, residence or second residence is not subject to the passive loss rule. This holds true even if the taxpayer rents out the residence. (See chapter 3 for a discussion of the new restrictions on deductions for home mortgage interest.)

NOTE: Although there is an exception for residence interest, other residence-related deductions are subject to the passive loss restrictions if the taxpayer rents out the home and does not actively participate in his "rental business." This can happen if a management agent handles all aspects of the business, including approval of tenants, as is the case with some "rent-pooled" vacation homes.

How the passive-loss rule works. To begin with, a taxpayer must satisfy the at-risk rules for real estate (which are discussed later in this chapter) and the limitations on deductions for interest on investment loans (discussed in Chapter 3). Deductions disallowed because the taxpayer's at-risk amount is insufficient are suspended by the at-risk rules. Such deductions become subject to the passive loss rules only if the taxpayer's at-risk amount increases in future years. Similar rules apply to interest subject to the investment-interest limitations.

Worse yet, a taxpayer's at-risk amount is reduced by losses allowed under the at-risk rules even if the losses are suspended by the passive loss rules. Similarly, a taxpayer's basis is reduced by deductions, such as depreciation, even if the deductions are not usable currently because of the passive loss rules.

Losses from passive activities can offset only passive activity income and cannot shelter "active" income such as salary. "Portfolio income" generated by the activity or earned by the taxpayer is not passive income and cannot be offset by passive losses. "Portfolio income" consists of: (1) interest, dividends and royalties (unless earned in the ordinary course of a trade or business) and (2) gain or loss on the sale of property that generates portfolio income or is held for investment. Income (for example, interest) earned on working capital is treated as portfolio income.

Special rules. A closely held C corporation (other than a personal-service corporation) may use passive losses and credits to offset its "net active income." This is taxable income of the company figured without regard to passive income or loss or portfolio income. And if a taxpayer becomes materially involved in what had been a passive activity, the taxpayer may use suspended losses to offset the activity's income, even though his or her interest is no longer passive.

Any tax credit generated by a passive activity (other than foreign tax credits) may offset only the tax attributable to passive income. That's the excess of the tax owed on all income less the tax that would be owed on non-passive-source income (passive-source credits are disregarded in both cases).

Allocations. A taxpayer must allocate income, deductions and credits among passive and active elements. And if the taxpayer owns several passive activities, he or she must prorate suspended losses and credits among the activities.

Example. During 1987, AB General Partnership operates an investment counseling business out of one floor of a three-story building that it owns. AB net leases the other two floors to a commercial tenant. Also, AB has portfolio income from dividends and interest, as well as a passive interest in an income-producing farm.

With that set of facts, the partners can use two-thirds of the building's deductions to offset rental income and income from the farm. Any excess deductions from the rented portion of the building cannot be used to shelter portfolio income or income from the counseling business. Since the remaining one-third of the building's deductions are allocable to a business in which the partners materially participate, it is not subject to the passive loss rule.

Note, however, that a different rule applies had AB been organized as a closely held C corporation. AB could use excess deductions from the apartment building to shelter its net active income.

Suspended losses and credits. They may be carried forward (but not back) and used to offset future years' passive-source income. A suspended loss is allowed in full when the entire interest is sold to a third party. Suspended losses (and any loss on the sale) are deductible against income in the following order: any gain recognized on the transaction; net income or gain from passive activities; and any other income or gain. In the case of an installment sale, passive losses become available as the buyer makes payments. Losses are freed up in the same ratio that gain recognized each year bears to the total gain on the sale.

Credits vanish. The passive loss rule is designed to limit writeoffs to real economic losses. Therefore, any unused suspended credits are not allowed when a passive activity is sold. In other words, the credits vanish into thin air.

Suspended losses are not freed up by:

● A change in the form of ownership (for instance, the tax-free transfer of a proprietorship interest to an S corporation),

● A like-kind exchange (except to the extent of taxable "boot," that is, other property, such as cash), or

● A partial disposition of a passive activity.

The sale of one passive activity by an entity that owns several releases suspended losses, but this doesn't do a limited partner any good. He cannot tap suspended losses until he has sold his entire interest in the limited partneship.

Other transfers. Any suspended losses remaining at the taxpayer's death are allowed as deductions on the taxpayer's final return to the extent they exceed the gain he or she would have recognized on sale.

Example. At the time of Joan Smith's death, her limited partnership interest has a basis of $10,000 and a value of $20,000. Assume she holds $15,000 of suspended losses. Of that $15,000, $5,000 may be deducted on her final return (suspended losses minus $10,000 gain she would have recognized on a sale).

Assume, instead, that suspended losses are $10,000 or less. Here, nothing is deductible.

In the case of a gift by a taxpayer of his or her entire interest in a passive activity, the donee's basis is increased by any suspended losses. If the interest is subsequently sold at a loss, however, the donee's basis is limited to the fair market value on the date the gift was made.

Limited relief for real estate. The new law gives some relief to an individual (but not to a corporation) who actively participates in a rental real estate activity. A person can offset non-passive income, such as salary, with losses and credits (in deduction equivalents) from his or her "active" real estate interests of up to $25,000 ($12,500 for marrieds filing separate returns). The deduction equivalent of a low-income housing credit (which is discussed later in this chapter) counts in full towards the $25,000 limit, whether or not the taxpayer is actively involved in the activity. The deduction equivalent of credits is the amount which, if allowed as a deduction, would reduce tax by an amount equal to the credit.

The special break for low-income housing credits applies only (for the original credit compliance period) to property placed in service prior to 1990. However, if the property is placed in service prior to 1992, the special break applies if 10% or more of the total low-income housing project costs are incurred before 1990.

Example. A taxpayer is an active participant in a real estate venture that produces $20,000 credits in 1988, but no deductions or income. Assume his taxable income is $70,000. In that event, he may claim a $7,000 credit for 1988. This is because for someone in a 28% tax bracket, $25,000 of deductions creates a tax savings of $7,000. The $13,000 balance of this credit is suspended by the passive loss rule.

Phase-out of $25,000 allowance. For joint filers, the $25,000 allowance is phased out on a 2-for-1 basis when adjusted gross income, figured without regard to passive losses, exceeds $100,000 ($50,000 for marrieds filing separately). Thus, there is no allowance at all once adjusted gross income exceeds $150,000 ($75,000 for marrieds filing separately).

In the case of credits from qualifying rehabilitations of buildings (discussed in the next section of this chapter) and low-income housing projects (discussed after rehabilitation projects), the $25,000 allowance (in deduction equivalents) is reduced by 50% when adjusted gross income, figured without regard to passive losses, exceeds $200,000 ($100,000 for marrieds filing separately). Thus, there's no credit once adjusted gross income exceeds $250,000 ($125,000 for marrieds filing separately).

Active participation standard for rental real estate. This standard is more liberal than the material participation standard that applies to other activities. All that's required is that the taxpayer or his or her spouse participate in a bona fide sense. For example, making management decisions, such as approving tenants and repairs, is sufficient even if an agent handles the day-to-day affairs of the real estate rental activity. However, a taxpayer cannot be an active participant if he is a limited partner or holds a less than 10% interest in the real estate deal.

Working interests in oil and gas properties. There is a complete exemption from the passive loss rule for a taxpayer who holds a working interest in an oil and gas property. It makes no difference whether or not he materially participates in the activity. A working interest is one that is burdened with the cost of developing and operating the property. Typical characteristics: responsibility for authorizing expenses; receiving periodic reports about drilling, completion and expected production; the possession of voting rights and rights to continue operations if the present operator steps out; a share in tort liability (for example, uninsured losses from a fire);

and some responsibility to share in additional costs.

A taxpayer whose liability is limited (for example, he holds a limited partnership interest or S corporation shares) is not treated as owning a working interest. Also specifically excepted from the definition of a working interest: rights to overriding royalties or production payments, and contract rights to extract or share in oil and gas profits without liability for a share of production costs.

Effective date. As a general rule, the passive loss rule applies to taxable years beginning after Dec. 31, 1986. But there's a five-year phase-in for passive activities that have started by the new law's enactment date or where there is a binding contract as of August 16, 1986. For tax years beginning in 1987, 35% of passive losses and credits is subject to the new rules. For tax years 1988, 1989, and 1990, the portion subject to the rules is 60%, 80% and 90%, respectively. For tax years 1991 and later, 100% of these passive losses and credits is subject to the new rules.

Example. In June of 1986, Dan Smith purchases a limited partnership interest in a cattle deal. In January of 1987, he buys a limited partnership interest in a farm. For 1987, the ventures produce $70,000 of deductions, but no income

($56,000 for the cattle deal and $14,000 from the farm). Here's how things work out for 1987:

Loss subject to phase-in (loss from activity
held on enactment date) $56,000
Loss not subject to phase in (loss acquired
after the law's effective date) 14,000
$70,000

Amount subject to passive loss rule
(1) $56,000 × .35 . . . $19,600
(2) $14,000 × 100% . . . . . .
. . . . 14,000
Total suspended losses . . . . .
. . . . $33,600   (33,600)
Deductible losses
. . . . $36,400

AT-RISK RULES EXTENDED TO REAL ESTATE SHELTERS

The at-risk rules prevent individuals and certain closely held corporations from deducting losses in excess of their actual economic investment (essentially, cash invested plus borrowed amounts on which there is personal liability) in specified activities. But under prior law, the at-risk rules did not apply to real estate investments. That among other things allowed investors to claim depreciation on the cost of a building, even though their investment was substantially financed by a nonrecourse (no personal liability) mortgage.

The new law extends the at-risk rules to the activity of holding real estate. The revised rules apply to losses attributable to property acquired after 1986.

Losses are deductible only to the extent of the amount the taxpayer has placed at risk, that is, the amount the taxpayer could actually lose by engaging in the activity. The at-risk amount includes cash contributions to the activity, the adjusted basis of other property contributed to the activity, as well as borrowed amounts used in the activity for which the taxpayer is personally liable, or has pledged property not used in the activity as security for repayment of the borrowed amounts. Generally, a person is not considered at risk where he or she is not personally liable for repayment of the debt (the borrowed amounts are nonrecourse loans) or the lender has an interest other than as a creditor in the activity.

Exception for third party nonrecourse financing. There is an important exception to these new rules that extend the at-risk rules to real estate activities. Taxpayers are considered to be at risk where they use arm's length, third party commercial financing secured solely by real property used in the activity, even though the lender has an equity interest in the property. Consequently, they are allowed to deduct losses to the extent of such financing. This exception, however, is inapplicable when the third party lender is (1) related to the taxpayer; (2) the seller of the property or someone related to the seller; or (3) a person who is paid a fee with respect to the taxpayer's investment in the property. For the exception to apply, the terms of the loan must be commercially reasonable and substantially similar to loans made to unrelated parties. The net effect of this exception is that a taxpayer's loss writeoffs can continue to exceed his at-risk amount even though he purchases real estate with nonrecourse debt, provided he does not obtain the nonrecourse financing from the seller or a promoter.

Special rule for partnerships. A partnership's nonrecourse financing can increase a partner's (including a limited partner's) amount at risk. But this is so only when the financing is qualified nonrecourse financing with respect to both the partner and the partnership. The amount the partners are treated at risk cannot be more than the total amount of the qualified nonrecourse financing at the partnership level.

REHABILITATION TAX CREDIT

The new law replaces the three-tier investment tax credit of 15% to 25% for the expenses of rehabilitating old buildings and certified historic structures with a two-tier credit of 10% to 20% for qualified rehab expenses. The revised credit percentage is 20% for rehabbing certified historic structures (those that meet one of several definitions of historic property or are located in registered historic districts) and 10% for rehabbing buildings, other than historic structures, built before 1936 (that is, at least 50 years old).

As under prior law, the credit for rehabbing historic structures applies to both residential and nonresidential buildings, while the credit for rehabbing buildings applies only to nonresidential buildings.

Basis adjustment. The basis of the rehabbed building is reduced by the full amount of the credit taken. This full basis adjustment applies to both the 10% and 20% rehab credit, instead of only a 50% reduction for historic structures.

When the changes become effective. Generally, the new rules for rehab credits apply to property placed in service after 1986. There are, however, transitional rules that are available generally for property placed in service after 1986, but before 1994, in the case of property that is acquired and undergoing rehab pursuant to a pre-March 2, 1986 contract. Property that qualified under a transitional rule and is placed in service after 1986 is eligible for reduced credits (25% to 20%, 20% to 13% and 15% to 10%), and a full basis adjustment.

LOW-INCOME HOUSING TAX CREDIT

Prior law favored low-income housing with a provision that allowed investors to write off the cost of rehabilitating low-income housing over only 15 years, compared to 19 for commercial real estate. This preferential treatment comes to an end at the close of 1986.

The Tax Reform Act authorizes three new tax credits for owners of low-income housing that, as a general rule, is put in service after 1986 and before 1990. The new credits are claimed over a 10-year period.

The first two credits are available on both newly constructed and newly rehabilitated properties. For property placed in service in 1987, the annual credit is generally 9% of the owner's expenditures. However, if the construction is financed with tax-exempt bonds or similar Federal subsidies, the credit is 4% per year. Expenditures must exceed $2,000 per unit.

The third credit is 4% each year for 10 years on the cost of acquiring existing low-income housing. The property must not have been previously placed in service within 10 years. Rehabilitation expenditures on such property can qualify for one of the other credits.

REAL ESTATE INVESTMENT TRUSTS (REITs)

The new law makes a number of changes in the rules for real estate investment trusts (REITs). These changes apply to taxable years beginning after 1986.

There is relief from certain shareholder and income and asset requirements for the first year that an entity otherwise qualifies as a REIT, as well as for the first year after a REIT receives new equity capital. Also, REITs now can hold assets in wholly owned subsidiaries. A modified definition of rents from real property permits REITs to perform certain services themselves, rather than using independent contractors for those services. The definitions of rents from real property and of interest now include rent or interest that is based on the net income of the tenant or debtor, but only if such net income is based substantially on amounts that would be treated as rents from real property if received directly by the REIT. REITs must distribute 95% of their income. They are relieved of this requirement when they have certain types of income that are not accompanied by the receipt of cash, though they must pay tax on undistributed amounts. Additionally, there is an expansion of the safe harbor that allows REITs to avoid the tax on prohibited transactions, a modification of the amount of capital gains dividends that may be paid and elimination of a penalty for deficiency dividends.

8
RETIREMENT PLANS

CUTBACK OF IRA DEDUCTIONS

The Tax Reform Act restricts deductions allowed individuals for money placed in Individual Retirement Accounts, starting with returns for 1987 to be filed in 1988. The allowable deduction depends upon whether a person is covered by a pension plan at work and the amount of his or her adjusted gross income (AGI).

NOTE: A person is considered to be "covered" by a pension plan as soon as he or she qualifies to participate in it, which may be immediately after starting work. This holds true even though an employee is not yet *vested,* which means the right that person acquires when he or she works at a place long enough to become entitled to receive a specified pension upon retirement.

Individuals not covered by employer pension plans. The Tax Act retains the existing rules for these individuals. Consequently, a working person remains entitled to deduct contributions to an IRA of up to $2,000 each year. Married couples who both work and are without pension coverage are able to deduct up to $4,000. A joint filer with a nonworking spouse can establish separate IRAs and deduct an additional $250, for a total deduction of up to $2,250. Interest, dividends and other earnings on funds in an account build up free of taxes until the funds are withdrawn.

Individuals covered by employer pension plans. The full deduction of up to $2,000 remains available when AGI (before a reduction for deductible IRA contributions) is less than $25,000 for a single person and $40,000 for a married couple filing jointly if either spouse has a pension plan. There is a phasing out of the $2,000 deduction, that is, only a partial deduction allowed when AGI is between $25,000 and $35,000 for a single person and between $40,000 and $50,000 for a couple filing jointly.

For each five dollars of AGI above $25,000 for a single person and $40,000 for a joint filer, the allowable IRA deduction decreases by one dollar. That means that only a partial deduction is allowed.

Take, for instance, a single person who is covered by a pension plan and has an AGI of $30,000. There is a $1,000 cap on the IRA deduction, as that person's AGI is half-way between the phase-out figures of $25,000 and $35,000. Similarly, the cap for a joint filer with an AGI of $45,000 and a nonworking spouse is $1,000, plus $125 for a spousal IRA, for a total of

$1,125. If both spouses work, they are able to deduct $1,000 apiece, for a total of $2,000.

A special rule gives a deduction of $200 for someone whose AGI falls within the last $1,000 of the phase-out range. Assume, for example, that a single person has an AGI of $34,500. The allowable deduction is $200, even though there would otherwise be a $100 cap.

The Tax Act bars any deduction for contributions to an IRA by a person covered by a pension plan when AGI exceeds $35,000 for a single person and $50,000 for joint filers. There is, however, a tax break for an individual who is ineligible to make deductible contributions. He or she has the option to make nondeductible contributions of as much as $2,000 or $2,250 and defer taxes on the earnings from such contributions until withdrawals begin.

To avoid being taxed twice, after-tax, nondeductible contributions to an IRA are not again taxed upon withdrawal. Only earnings are taxed upon withdrawal.

TAX SAVING BENEFITS OF AN IRA DEDUCTION

If you are in the 28% bracket, a deductible contribution of $2,000 reduces your tax by $560.

Had you merely invested $2,000 of income in another type of investment, this would be the equivalent of investing only $1,440 after taking into account tax on the $2,000.

	Taxes saved by deductions	
Contribution	Tax Bracket	
years	15%	28%
10	$3,000	$ 5,600
20	6,000	11,200
30	9,000	16,800

MAKING NONDEDUCTIBLE IRA CONTRIBUTIONS

Even though you may not deduct an IRA contribution because you have company coverage or too much income, it may be advisable to invest in an IRA. Income earned on an IRA account accumulates tax free until withdrawn.

$2,000 invested annually for	Rate of interest compounded daily	
	8% gives you	12% gives you
10 years	$ 32,100	$ 48,150
20 years	$104,346	$156,519
30 years	$266,942	$400,413

You may withdraw nondeductible contributions without penalty or tax as they are a return of your principal. If over the years you make deductible and nondeductible IRA contributions, you must distinguish between the different IRA accounts so that you do not confuse the separate tax consequences of each type of account.

IRA WITHDRAWAL PENALTY

The penalty for an early withdrawal from an IRA remains 10%. The penalty applies to withdrawals before age 59½, except for death or disability.

The Tax Reform Act creates another exception. Under the new rules, IRA withdrawals taken after 1986 as a life annuity are not subject to the early withdrawal penalty.

NEW IRA INVESTMENT

Starting in 1987, you can invest your IRA funds in U.S. gold and silver coins. The prohibition on investing in other collectibles remains in place.

LUMP-SUM WITHDRAWALS FROM RETIREMENT PLANS

The Tax Reform Act curbs special tax breaks for lump-sum withdrawals from retirement plans. These restrictions apply to withdrawals after 1986.

Prior law authorizes ten-year averaging for certain lump-sum withdrawals from plans and capital gains treatment on withdrawals attributable to pre-1974 years.

The Act generally replaces ten-year averaging with five-year averaging. However, you are entitled to elect five-year averaging only once—and then only after you reach age 59½.

There is a phasing out of capital gains treatment over six years. Capital gains treatment remains available for the following percentages of the withdrawal: 100% in 1987, 95% in 1988, 75% in 1989, 50% in 1990 and 25% in 1991.

The Act authorizes special relief from the new rules for an employee who was at least age 50 on January 1, 1986. The employee can choose between ten-year averaging using 1986 tax rates and five-year averaging using the new tax rates. Also, the employee can disregard the six-year phase-out for capital gains treatment. The capital gain is taxed at a flat 20%. An employee who elects this special relief cannot again elect lump-sum treatment after reaching age 59½.

401(k) PLANS

A cash or deferred plan (known as a 401(k) plan after the section of the Internal Revenue Code that authorizes such an arrangement) allows employees to defer up to 25% of their compensation to a profit-sharing plan, where the money grows without current tax.

The Tax Reform Act limits the amounts that can be deferred, starting with returns for 1987 to be filed in 1988. The maximum deferral drops from $30,000 to $7,000. The $7,000 cap is adjusted annually to offset inflation.

THREE-YEAR RECOVERY OF COST RULE REPEALED

There is something in the law known as a "three-year cost recovery" rule. This rule applies to pensioners, mainly former government employees, who contributed to their pension plans and receive benefits equal to their own contributions within three years after they start collecting. Under this rule, they are relieved of taxes on their benefits until they recover all of their own contributions. After that, all of their benefits are taxable.

The Tax Reform Act retroactively repeals that rule as of July 1, 1986. Workers who retire after July 1 are taxed as soon as they retire on the portion of their benefits attributable to employer contributions.

9
EMPLOYEE TAX BENEFITS

DEDUCTIBLE HEALTH INSURANCE FOR SELF-EMPLOYEDS

The law allows an exclusion from an employee's income for an employer's contribution to a plan that provides accident or health benefits. Prior law, though, failed to provide a similar break for self-employed individuals who operate their business as sole proprietorships or partnerships.

To narrow this distinction between self-employeds and owners of incorporated businesses, the 1986 Tax Reform Act provides partial relief for self-employeds for a three-year period, starting with returns for 1987 to be filed in 1988 and ending with returns for 1989 to be filed in 1990. They can deduct 25% of payments for health insurance for a self-employed individual and that individual's spouse and dependents. This special deduction for health insurance is not subject to the new 7.5% of adjusted gross income floor beneath medical-expense deductions (the new floor for medical expenses is discussed in chapter 3).

The health-insurance deduction, though, is subject to several limitations. No deduction is allowed to the extent health-insurance payments exceed a self-employed's earned income for the taxable year. Nor is any deduction allowed for any taxable year for which the self-employed is eligible to participate in a subsidized accident and health plan provided by an organization that employs (whether on a full- or part-time basis) the self-employed individual or that individual's spouse. Also, no deduction is allowed unless the self-employed provides coverage under one or more accident or health plans for all employees. Those plans must satisfy nondiscrimination rules, that is, the benefits available to the self-employed individual are available to the individuals's employees on a nondiscriminatory basis.

The deduction for health insurance payments is claimed on Form 1040 as an "above-the-line" adjustment, that is, a subtraction from gross income to arrive at adjusted gross income, rather than as an itemized deduction. Thus, the health-insurance deduction is available even to an individual who uses the standard deduction.

No additional breaks are allowed, however, for health-insurance payments when it comes to calculating medical-expenses deductions or self-employment taxes. Any payment deductible as health coverage for a self-employed individual does not count for purposes of determining whether that individual is entitled to deduct medical expenses because they total more than the nondeductible floor of 7.5% for medical expenses.

Nor does deductible health coverage count in computing net earnings from self-employment for Social Security tax purposes. Put another way, deductible coverage does not reduce the earnings amount used to compute the self-employment tax on Schedule SE of Form 1040.

EMPLOYEE ACHIEVEMENT AWARDS

The 1986 Tax Reform Act spells out when employee awards count as reportable income and when they do not. The Act authorizes an exclusion from income, that is, tax-free treatment for employees who receive what the law refers to as "employee achievement awards." These are awards for length of service or safety achievement. The new rules set separate limits of $400 and $1,600 on the amounts that employees can exclude, as well as limits on amounts that employers can deduct. What follows is a closer look at the new rules that take affect starting with returns for 1987 to be filed in 1988.

Employee achievement award defined. It is an item of tangible personal property, such as a watch, that an employer transfers to an employee for length of service achievement or for safety achievement. The property must be awarded as part of a meaningful presentation and under conditions and circumstances that do not create a significant likelihood that the payment is disguised compensation.

Congressional committee reports provide examples of disguised-compensation situations. They include employee awards made at the time of annual salary adjustments, as a substitute for a prior program of awarding cash bonuses or in a way that discriminates in favor of highly paid employees.

NOTE: Only tangible personal property qualifies. No exclusion, say Congressional committee reports, for awards of cash, gift certificates or equivalent items.

Length-of-service awards. The new law bars an exclusion for an award when an employee receives it during his or her first five years of employment for the employer making the award or when he or she has previously received an award during that year or any of the preceding four years, unless the previous award qualifies under a different exclusion for de minimis fringes, that is, benefits so small that they are administratively impractical to tax.

Safety-achievement awards. There is no exclusion for an award made to an employee not in the category of eligible employees or if, during the year, the employer previously made safety awards to more than 10% of the eligible employees.

Which employees are eligible and which ones ineligible? All are eligible, except for managers, administrators, clerical workers and other professional employees. Why not these people? Because, according to Congressional committee reports, they do not engage in work involving significant safety concerns.

Limitations on deductions allowed employers. As a general rule, there is a $400 limit on the deduction by an employer for all safety and length-of-service awards (other than qualified plan awards) provided to the same employee during the taxable year. There is, however, a ceiling of $1,600 on the deduction for all qualified plan awards (QPAs), whether for safety or length of service, when an employer makes one or more QPAs to the same employee during the taxable year.

NOTE: There is no parlaying of the separate $400/$1,6000 limits, note Congressional committee reports. In addition to these separate limits, the $1,600 limit applies in the aggregate when an employee receives one or more QPAs during the year and also one or more awards that are not QPAs. That means no adding together of the $400 and $1,600 limits to allow deductions exceeding an aggregate of $1,600 for awards to the same employee in a taxable year. In the case of a partnership, the $400 and $1,600 limits apply to the partnership, as well as to each partner.

Qualified plan award. The new law says it means an employee achievement award provided under a qualified award plan. The plan must be an established written plan or program of the taxpayer that does not discriminate in favor of highly compensated employees as to eligibility or benefits.

Average-cost ceiling on awards. QPA treatment is unavailable if the average cost per recipient of all achievement awards made under all qualified award plans of the employer during the taxable year exceeds $400. For purposes of the average-cost calculation, do not include QPAs of nominal value, that is, they are not to be added into the total of award costs under the plan.

When the cost of a QPA exceeds $1,600, its entire cost is to be added into the total of award costs under the plan. It is immaterial that the allowable deduction for such cost is only $1,600 or less, note Congressional committee reports.

Limitation on amounts excludable by employees. The fair market value of an achievement award is fully excludable by the employee when the cost of the award is fully deductible by the employer under the $400/$1,600 limits.

NOTE. The deduction-limit amount for a tax-exempt employer, such as a school or library, is the amount that would be deductible if the employer were not tax exempt, according to Congressional committee reports.

Example: Lady Godiva Accessories awards a crystal bowl as a length-of-service award (other than a QPA) to June Brown. For the year in question, Accessories makes no other safety or length-of-service award to June; nor did it make a length-of-service award to her during the previous four years. The bowl cost Accessories $375. Its fair market value is $415. June can exclude the $415.

Excess deduction awards. An employee cannot exclude the entire fair market value of an achievement award when its cost exceeds the amount allowable as a deduction by an employer because of the $400/$1,600 limits. There is however, a cap on how much an employee has to include in income.

The includable amount is the *greater* of: (1) the portion of the cost to the employer that is not allowable as an employer deduction, but not an amount in excess of the award's fair market value *or* (2) the difference between the award's fair market value and the maximum allowable employer deduction. An employee can exclude the remaining portion of the award's fair market value.

Example: Consolidated Enterprises pays $500 for a watch (not a QPA) that goes as a safety award to John Green, an eligible employee. For the year in question, Consolidated made no achievement awards to John and did not previously make safety awards to more than 10% of the eligible employees. Consolidated's deduction is limited to $400. John must include as income, the greater of (1) $100, which is the difference between the watch's cost of $500 and Consolidated's $400 deduction limit, or (2) the difference between the watch's fair market value and Consolidated's $400 deduction. With an assumed fair market value of $475, John includes $100. With a fair market value of $600, he includes $200.

De minimus fringes. The new law does not change the exclusion from income for de minimus fringes, that is, benefits so small that they are administratively impractical to tax. Consequently, there is an exclusion for an employee award when its fair market value, after considering the frequency with which the employer provides similar benefits to its employees, is so small that it is impractical to tax.

Traditional retirement gifts ordinarily treated as de minimus fringes. Congressional committee reports clarify whether the exclusion for de minimus fringes provides relief from taxes for traditional retirement gifts received by an employee who retires after lengthy service and cannot qualify under the exclusion for a length-of-service award because the employee received such an award within the previous four years. In determining whether such a retirement gift passes muster as a de minimus fringe, Congress wants the IRS to consider how long the employee worked for the employer.

Example. Susan White receives a gold watch on retirement after 25 years of employment. Her watch can qualify as a de minimus fringe. It does not matter that other watches that she previously received did not qualify as de minimus fringes.

NEW NONDISCRIMINATION RULES FOR FRINGE BENEFITS

The 1986 Tax Reform Act establishes comprehensive nondiscrimination rules for certain statutory employee benefit plans. Statutory plans are employer-provided plans that offer fringe benefits to employees and are authorized by a specific section of the Internal Revenue Code.

Under the new rules, there are nondiscrimination tests for eligibility and benefits. These tests have to be met for each benefit and can be satisfied on a line of business or operating unit basis. In general, the tests apply to health plans, group-term life insurance plans and dependent care assistance programs.

The new rules apply to plan years that begin after 1987. However, if the IRS has not yet issued explanatory regulations by that time, then the rules apply to the earlier of plan years that begin at least three months after the regulations are issued or plan years that begin after 1988.

LEGAL SERVICES EXCLUSION

The new law extends for two years through 1987 the exclusion for employer-paid group legal services that expired at the end of 1985. Under this exclusion, employees are not taxable on employer payments for legal services, or the value of services received under a qualified group legal services plan.

EDUCATIONAL ASSISTANCE EXCLUSION

A law allowing tax-free treatment for an employer's payment of educational costs under a nondiscriminatory plan expired at the end of 1985. The new law extends the exclusion for two years through 1987 and increases the overall limitation on the annual tax-free benefit from $5,000 to $5,250 per employee.

You will owe no tax in 1986 on your employer's payment of up to $5,250 for tuition, books, fees, supplies and equipment for any courses, including courses that are not job related, provided they do not involve sports, games or hobbies. Benefits above $5,250 are taxable.

CAMPUS LODGING

The new law sets up rules for tax-free treatment of campus lodging provided by universities, colleges and other educational organizations to their employees. Under these rules, an employee is not taxed on the value of qualified campus lodging if the rent that the employee pays is at least equal to 5% of the appraised value of the lodging or the average of rentals paid (other than by employees or students) to the educational institution for comparable housing, whichever is the lesser figure.

Qualified campus lodging means lodging furnished by an educational institution to an employee, spouse or dependents for use as a residence. The lodging must be located on, or in proximity to, the institution's campus.

The new rules apply to taxable years beginning after 1985.

ACCRUED VACATION PAY

The new law limits the deduction for additions to the earned vacation pay accrual amount. For taxable years beginning after 1986, the deduction is limited to amounts paid during the employer's current taxable year or within 8½ months (rather than the 12 months allowed under prior law) after the close of the taxable year in which the vacation pay was earned.

LIMIT ON EXCLUSION FOR DEPENDENT CARE ASSISTANCE

The new law limits the exclusion, that is, tax-free treatment for employer-provided dependent care assistance. The exclusion is $5,000 a year ($2,500 for a married person filing separately), starting with returns for 1987 to be filed in 1988.

Previously, the exclusion was limited to the amount of earned income. Consequently, the change constitutes a cut in the amount of the exclusion for most persons.

The new law also explains how to determine the amount excludable as an assistance benefit when child care is provided at a facility on the employer's premises. In general, the amount excludable is the value of services provided to employees who actually use the facility.

10
BUSINESS TRAVEL AND
ENTERTAINMENT EXPENSES

OVERVIEW OF NEW TRAVEL AND ENTERTAINMENT RULES

The 1986 Tax Reform Act makes sweeping changes in the rules for business travel and entertainment expenses, starting with returns for 1987 to be filed in 1988. These changes are discussed in more detail in the sections that follow.

● A business meal is deductible only if it is "directly related to" or "associated with" the active conduct of your business. In other words, you have to talk business at the table or have the meal before or after a substantial and bona fide business discussion. Previously, you could deduct a "quiet business meal"—one held in an atmosphere conducive to business—even though business was not actually discussed.

● As a general rule, the new law limits the deduction for otherwise allowable business meals and entertainment costs to 80% of their actual cost. The new 20% disallowance rule on meals also applies to meals while away from home overnight on business.

● Deductions for tickets to entertainment events cannot, as a general rule, exceed their face value. Also, there are new restrictions on writeoffs for luxury skybox rentals at sports events. Moreover, tickets and skybox rentals are subject to the 20% disallowance rule. But an exception to the face-value requirement retains a 100% deduction for tickets to a sports event when these tests are met: the entire proceeds go to a charitable organization and the event (for instance, a charity golf outing) utilizes volunteers for substantially all the work performed in carrying out the event.

● Deductions for what the law refers to as luxury water travel come under new restrictions. Generally, the ceiling is twice the highest Federal government travel allowance rate times the number of days in transit.

Other travel crackdowns are discussed in chapter 3. A key change concerns unreimbursed employee expenses for business travel, transportation and entertainment. Those expenses are now categorized as miscellaneous itemized deductions and are subject to a 2% of adjusted gross income "floor." Deductions are no longer allowed for travel as a form of education, certain types of travel on behalf of charitable organizations, and attending investment-related seminars and conventions.

Let's take a closer look at these wide-ranging revisions.

QUIET BUSINESS MEALS NO LONGER DEDUCTIBLE

The Tax Reform Act ends deductions for the most common method of business entertaining—"quiet business meals" that are for goodwill purposes only. Previously, you could deduct the cost of goodwill wining and dining of business associates in restaurants, bars, hotels and other places with atmospheres conducive to business discussions. It made no difference that you actually discussed not a word of business before, during or after the entertaining. Starting with returns for 1987 to be filed in 1988, the tax break for quiet business meals is no longer available. Like other types of entertainment, business meals are deductible only if they are "directly related to" or "associated with" the active conduct of a business.

Directly related test. For a business meal or entertainment outlay to pass this test, the main reason for the expense must be the active conduct of business. You need to show more than a general expectation of getting future income or some other specific business benefit (other than good will). But you need not prove that income or some other benefit actually resulted from the expense. You *do*, however, have to actually engage in business discussions during the meal or entertainment. If you did not talk business, it was for reasons beyond your control.

Associated with test. A meal or entertainment expense is deductible if it directly precedes or follows a substantial and bona fide business discussion on a subject associated with the active conduct of your business. If your business guest is from out of town, the meal or entertainment can take place the day before or after the business discussion. You do *not* have to discuss business during the meal. Under this test, a meal that is solely for good-will purposes is deductible, whether the dining is to obtain new business or to maintain an existing business relationship.

Other requirements. Besides the directly related and associated with tests, two other requirements must be met. The business meal or entertainment cannot, as under prior law, be lavish or extravagant under the circumstances. Also, there is a new "presence" requirement. The meal is deductible only if the taxpayer, or an employee of the taxpayer, is present.

Presence at meal. The requirement that there be a business discussion applies to all meals, except for someone eating alone while away from home overnight on business. The new rules bar a business-meal deduction unless one of those present is the taxpayer, an employee of the taxpayer, or, as explained below, an independent contractor (someone not an employee of the taxpayer) who is there on behalf of the taxpayer.

Example. The deduction is unavailable when the taxpayer reserves a table for a business dinner that is unattended by the taxpayer or an employer of the taxpayer. Similarly, no deduction is allowed when one of the parties to a contract negotiation buys dinner for the other parties, but does not attend the dinner. It makes no difference that the other parties discuss business while they break bread.

Presence requirement can be met by attendance of an independent contractor. The need for the taxpayer or an employee of the taxpayer to be present can be satisfied by the presence at the meal of an independent contractor, such as an attorney or accountant. The independent contractor must be someone who renders significant services on behalf of the taxpayer (other than attending meals on the taxpayer's behalf or providing service relating to meals) and attends the meal to perform those services. For purposes of the presence test, the meal-attending independent contractor is treated as an employee of the taxpayer.

Example. Recreational Company retains attorney Adams to represent it in the acquisition of Accessories Limited. Recreational pays for a dinner, attended by representatives of Accessories and by Adams, but not attended by any of its employees, at which the acquisition is discussed. *Result:* Recreational gets to deduct the dinner. Its deduction, however, is subject to that 20% disallowance rule.

NOTE: The entire cost of the meal does not become nondeductible when neither the taxpayer nor someone who represents attends the meal. The meal expense comes under the rules for business gifts. However, business gifts are subject to an annual limit of $25 per recipient.

No presence requirement when packaged gifts consumed. The new law relaxes "the presence" rule for taxpayers who transfer packaged food or beverage items, such as holiday turkeys, hams, fruitcakes or bottles of wine.

Example: Hank Ibsen sends a Thanksgiving turkey to his client, Hedda Gobbler. Hank gets a writeoff (subject to the $25 ceiling on deductions for gifts) for his present without being present when Hedda carves the bird.

DEDUCTIONS FOR MEALS AND ENTERTAINMENT LIMITED TO 80%

Generally, the new law places a limit of 80% of the actual cost on the deduction for meals and entertainment expenses, starting with returns for 1987 to be filed in 1988.

For example, if a taxpayer spends $100 for a business meal that was fully deductible under prior law, the amount of the allowable deduction is now reduced to $80 (or 80% of actual cost). This deduction curtailment also applies to meals while away from home overnight on business and to meals provided by employers on their premises for employees. The 20% disallowance rule is subject to certain important exceptions, for which a 100% deduction remains available. These exceptions are discussed below.

Expenses included and excluded from 20% disallowance rule. Besides meal and entertainment charges, expenses subject to the reduction rule include meal- or entertainment-related taxes and tips, cover charges for night club admissions, room rentals for dinners or cocktail parties and parking at sports arenas, but not transportation to and from business meals, such as cab fares to restaurants.

Example. The charge for a business meal, including beverages, comes to $50, plus $4 tax and $10 for tips. The amount of the deduction cannot exceed $51.20 (80% of $64). However, cab fare to the restaurant of $5, including tip, is 100% deductible.

Interplay of 20% reduction and other limitations. Congressional committee reports explain the interplay of the new 20% rule with the following:

• Restrictions on deductions for meal and entertainment expenses, such as a rule that disallows lavish and extravagant expenses and the new limitation of ticket deductions to face value (which is discussed below); and

• The new 2% floor on miscellaneous itemized deductions, such as unreimbursed expenses for meals and entertainment incurred by employees while traveling away from home and by outside salespersons. (See chapter 3 for a discussion of deductions for employee business expenses.)

Generally, taxpayers first have to apply the other restrictions on deductions for meal and entertainment expenses *before* they apply the 20% reduction. However, the 20% reduction applies *first* when there are separately stated meal and entertainment charges for what the law refers to as luxury water travel. This type of travel is subject to a new limitation that is explained below.

The 20% reduction also applies first when there are limitations such as the 2% floor on unreimbursed expenses for meals and entertainment incurred by employees while traveling away from home and by outside salespersons.

Example. A business related meal costs $100. Of this cost, $40 is disallowed as lavish and extravagant, which leaves $60. After the disallowance, the taxpayer subtracts 20% ($60 × 20% = $12), which results in an allowable deduction of $48 for the meal.

Example. Ms. Stowe, an outside salesperson for Legree Recreation, has an adjusted gross income of $70,000. Her miscellaneous itemized deductions include outside salesperson's expenses, of which $2,000 are for business meals away from home for which she has not been reimbursed by Legree. Ms. Stowe must first reduce her meals deduction by $400 ($2,000 × 20%). Next, she adds the remaining $1,600 for meals to her outside salesperson's expenses before reducing her total outside salesperson's expenses by $1,400 ($70,000 x 2%).

Example. Green, a dress manufacturer, pays a scalper $100 for a $20 ticket to a performance by Poi George And His Hawaiian Hotshots. The ticket writeoff is reduced from the $100 payment to the $20 face value before a further reduction of $4 ($20 × 20%), leaving an allowable deduction of $16.

Meal expenses during a tax-deductible, work-related move. Prior law allowed a 100% deduction for meals consumed during a work-related move. The new law imposes the 20% reduction on those meals, including separately charged meals consumed while traveling by luxury water transportation to a new work site (see below).

Exceptions to the 20% disallowance rule. There is no disallowance and a 100% deduction remains available for meal and entertainment expenses that qualify under one of these exceptions:

● Compensation. The new law retains a full deduction for expenses when their full value is (1) taxable compensation to the recipients, whether or not they are employees, or (2) shielded from taxation by the exclusions for small or de minimis fringe benefits that are impractical to tax or for subsidized eating facilities.

Example. A full deduction may be taken for packaged food or beverage items, such as employer-to-employee holiday gifts of turkeys, hams, fruitcakes or bottles of wine that are considered excludable fringes.

● Reimbursements of business meals and entertainment. When expenses are reimbursed, as for instance to an employee by his or her employer, the 20% reduction applies to the amount claimed as a deduction by the one who reimburses, not the one who is reimbursed.

Example. Ms. Adler, a salesperson for Holmes Limited, has a luncheon meeting with a customer to discuss a sales contract. She pays $50 for the lunch and is reimbursed by Holmes, whose deduction is trimmed to $40 ($50 × 80%).

● Employer-provided recreation. Employers suffer no 20% reduction when they pay for recreational, social or similar facilities or activities for employees generally. Examples include year-end holiday parties or summer outings for employees and their spouses.

● Items available to public. Samples or promotional items made available to the public are fully deductible.

Example. Able Audio pays $500 for baseball tickets that it offers to the first 50 people who visit its retail store on January 2, or buy something from it during a sale. The full $500 is deductible.

Example. Stern's Liquor store can claim the entire cost of wine samples sipped by potential purchasers of the kind of wine the merchant offers, as well as what it pays for associated wine testing costs, such as cheese and crackers provided with the wine to demonstrate its suitability for particular meals.

● Sports tickets. There is no 20% reduction for tickets to a sporting event that qualifies as a charitable fundraiser.

When is an event a charitable fundraiser? The tickets are fully deductible only if the event passes a three-step test: First, its primary purpose is to benefit a tax-exempt charitable organization, such as a church or school. Second, the entire net proceeds go to that charity. Third, it uses volunteers for substantially all of the work performed in carrying out the event.

This sporting-event exception covers the entire cost of a ticket package that includes seating at the event and related services, such as parking, use of entertainment areas, contestant positions and meals furnished at and as part of the event.

Exceptions to the exceptions on sporting events. Congressional committee reports specify that the fundraiser exception covers tickets to a charity golf outing. It matters not that the tournament offers prizes to participating golfers or uses paid concessionaires or security personnel.

No exception is allowed, however, for high school or college games. The 20% disallowance rule applies to tickets to football or basketball games or other similar scholastic events. Why does the new law decline to carve out an exception for school games? Because, according to Congressional committee reports, these games generally flunk the test for volunteers performing substantially all work when the institutions (or parties acting on their behalf) pay individuals to perform such services as coaching or recruiting.

● Meals and entertainment sold to customers. These items are fully deductible to the extent they are sold by a taxpayer in a bona fide transaction for an adequate and full consideration in money or money's worth. For example, a restaurant gets to deduct the full cost of meals provided paying customers.

● Qualifying banquet meetings during 1987 and 1988. There is a full deduction during 1987 and 1988 for the cost of a meal that is provided as an intergral part of a qualified banquet meeting, provided charges for the meal are not separately stated.

The two-year reprieve ends at the close of 1988. Starting January 1, 1989, qualified banquet meeting meals are subject to the 20% disallowance rule in the same way as other meals.

A qualified banquet meeting is a convention, seminar, annual meeting or similar business program that includes the meal. For the exception to apply for the two years mentioned, the banquet meeting must pass a three-step test: First, more than 50% of the participants at the meeting are away from home, that is, their travel expenses are deductible under the "away from home overnight" rule; second, at least 40 persons attend the banquet meeting; and third, the meal event is part of the banquet meeting and includes a speaker.

NOTE: There is no requirement that the at least 40 attendees be able to deduct their travel expenses under the overnight rule. Nor is it necessary for the attendees to remain awake during the speech.

TICKET DEDUCTIONS LIMITED TO FACE VALUE

The new law generally limits deductions for tickets to entertainment events to their face value, starting with returns for 1987 to be filed in 1988. The term "face value" includes any ticket tax.

According to Congressional committee reports, the face-value limitation bars these kinds of expenses:

● Payment to a scalper for a ticket (even if not otherwise disallowed under a different rule that prohibits a deduction for an illegal payment), for the part in excess of the ticket's face value; and

● Payment to a ticket agency for the part in excess of the ticket's face value.

Exception for tickets to charitable fundraisers. Under an exception to the face-value limitation, the full deduction remains available for tickets that sidestep the 20% disallowance rule because the tickets are for sporting events that are considered charitable fundraisers. A qualifying event must turn over the entire net proceeds to a charitable organization and use volunteers for substantially all the work performed in carrying out the event. See the discussion above of charitable fundraisers.

Example. Delphic Information Systems pays $100 for a $30 ticket to a charity golf outing. The full $100 is deductible. Delphic also pays a scalper $100 for a $40 ticket to a Broadway play. The allowable writeoff drops from the $100 payment to the $40 face value before, because of the 20% disallowance rule, there is an additional disallowance of $8, leaving a deduction of $32.

Problem for ticket agencies. According to Congressional committee reports, the face-value limitation applies to both illegal scalpers and legitimate ticket agencies. But local law allows these agencies to include their fees in the price they charge for tickets to plays, ball games and other events. Mandating like treatment for scalpers and agencies will adversely affect the ability of agencies to sell tickets to businesses.

Interplay of face-value limitation and 20% disallowance. Taxpayers must first apply the face-value limitation before they apply the 20% disallowance.

SKYBOX DEDUCTIONS RESTRICTED

In general, the Tax Reform Act sets a limit on deductions allowed for skybox rentals for more than one sporting event. The limitation applies to deductions for taxable years that start after 1986. For a taxpayer who reports on a calendar year basis, it is the taxable year that begins on January 1, 1987.

Under the Act, deductions for more-than-one-event rentals cannot exceed the sum of the face values of non-luxury box seat tickets for the number of seats in the box. In other words, the new law disallows part of the deduction for skyboxes.

The Act authorizes relief for skybox renters from the immediate impact of the partial disallowance of deductions. The disallowance of excess costs is gradually phased in over a three-year period, not taking full effect until taxable years that begin in 1989.

NOTE: The new restrictions are not applicable to deductions for *single-event rentals*. Those rentals remain deductible under the general rules for entertainment activities, including the 20% disallowance rule, which is explained above.

Skybox defined. Congressional committee reports say it is any private luxury box or other facility at a sports arena that is separated from other seating and is available at a higher price than the price applicable to other seating. Count as part of the box price all applicable expenses, such as rental of the facility, as well as separate charges for food and seating, though, as explained below, special relief is available for separately charged food.

When is a rental for more than one event? The face-value limitation comes into play only when a taxpayer rents a skybox at the same sports arena for more than one event. For example, a skybox rental for two World Series games in the same stadium is considered a two-event rental.

Treat as a more-than-one-event rental all rentals by a taxpayer in the same arena, along with any related rentals. Rentals are considered related when a taxpayer rents different skyboxes in the same stadium, whether pursuant to a single agreement or separate ones, or when the renters are related parties. Related rentals include skybox leases for different events by members of the same family, corporations with common ownership and otherwise unrelated taxpayers who make reciprocal arrangements to share skyboxes.

Exceptions. The face-value limitation does not bar deductions for these items:

● Separately stated charges for food or beverages; these charges are deductible under the general rules for entertainment expenses, including the 20% disallowance rule, which is discussed above; and

● The face values of non-luxury box seat tickets for the number of seats in the luxury box, subject, though, to further reduction under the 20% disallowance rule.

Example. In 1990, Icarus Airlines pays $500 to rent a skybox with five seats for two games at a stadium. Box seats (other than those in skyboxes) range in cost from $8 to $12 a seat. Icarus has a nondeductible excess cost of $380, which is the difference between $500 and $120 (5 seats times two games times $12). It is left with a deduction of $120, before a further reduction of $24 ($120 × 20%), leaving an allowable deduction of $96.

Icarus keeps its $96 deduction even though some seats go unused during the games. Nor does it matter whether the box payments nominally constitute seat payments or box rentals.

NOTE: Congress told the IRS to disregard the price charged for a non-luxury box seat that is inflated to allow the purchaser to circumvent the face-value limitation.

Example. Suppose that the stadium in the previous example seeks to boost box rentals by increasing the deduction allowed Icarus and other renters. The stadium reserves and charges $50 for a small group of seats that are not significantly better than the ones that sell for $12. Since the $50 figure is not genuine, it is disregarded and the deduction allowed Icarus (after the 20% disallowance) remains $96.

LUXURY WATER TRAVEL DEDUCTIONS LIMITED

As part of the crackdown on what Congress sees as expense account living, the new law generally limits deductions for business travelers who use ocean liners, cruise ships or other forms of what is categorized as "luxury water transportation." The limitation applies starting with returns for 1987 to be filed in 1988.

From now on, there is a cap on the writeoff allowed unhurried travelers who reach their business destinations by boating, rather than journeying on airplanes or other alternatives that are faster and less expensive than luxury water transportation. The deduction limit is twice the highest Federal government employee per diem travel allowance rate times the number of days in transit.

NOTE: There is no exemption from the per diem limitation for someone who uses luxury water transportation because of an illness or disability that rules out travel on an airplane.

Limitation defined. The allowable deduction per day on the boat cannot exceed twice "the highest amount generally allowable with respect to a day of travel to employees of the executive branch of the Federal Government while away from home but serving in the United States" times the days of luxury water travel. The applicable per diem amount generally is the highest travel amount for an area in the coterminous United States, disregarding any limited special exception, such as a higher limit authorized only for high-ranking executive personnel.

Example. Mr. Lang has to make a New York-to-London business trip. To ease the strain of travel across the Atlantic, he sails to London on a six-day voyage on the S.S. Luxurious. For the year in which he undertakes the voyage, the Federal per diem amount is $75. Therefore, the perdiem-limitation allows Lang to deduct no more than $900 ($150 per day × 6 days).

Interplay of 20% reduction rule for meals and entertainment and perdiem limitation for luxury water travel. Special rules apply when luxury water travel outlays include separately stated charges for meals and/or entertainment. Taxpayers must first apply the 20% reduction (which is discussed above) to those charges before they apply the per-diem limitation when using luxury water travel for business reasons. What if there are no separately stated charges? Taxpayers must allocate part of the total charge to meals or entertainment only if the amounts to be allocated are clearly identifiable.

Water travel on a work-related move. Congressional committee reports for the 1986 Tax Reform Act do not discuss the applicability of the per diem limitation and the 20% reduction for meals to a deduction for work-related moving expenses. However, both the per diem limitation and the 20% reduction for meals do apply to the luxury travel by water portion of the journey to a new work site.

Example. Ms. Vera Simpson makes a job transfer from London to Chicago. For the cross-Atlantic leg, Ms. Simpson takes an ocean liner. For the last leg, she drives to Chicago. *Result:* The per diem limitation applies to the Atlantic cruise, as does the 20% reduction rule to any separately charged cruise meals and to all meals consumed while driving.

Exceptions. The new law expressly bars application of the per diem rules to expenses that are allocable to conventions, seminars or other meetings on cruise ships. Therefore, the new law leaves unchanged the rules that allow deductions of up to $2,000 for cruise-ship conventions, provided the ship is a U.S. flagship and all ports of call are in the U.S. or its possessions.

Also, the exceptions for meals or entertainment from the water-travel, per diem limitation are the same as the exceptions from the 20% reduction rule. The exceptions (covered above in more detail in the discussion of the 20% reduction rule) are for:

● Compensation that is fully taxed to the recipient or an excludable fringe;

● Reimbursements;

● Employer-provided recreation;

● Items made available to the general public; and

● Meals and entertainment sold to customers.

NOTE: Chapter 3 discusses the deduction for moving expenses. The Act ended the classification of moving expenses as an "above-the-line" adjustment, that is, a subtraction from gross income to arrive at adjusted gross income that was deductible by individuals regardless of whether they itemized. Under the new rules, moving expenses are allowed only as an itemized deduction, which means that those expense are unavailable to persons who forego itemizing and use the standard deductions.

11
CORPORATE LAW CHANGES

CORPORATE TAX RATES DECREASED

The 1986 Tax Reform Act replaces the five step, graduated rate structure for corporations with a three step system. The revised rates of 15%, 25% and 34% apply to taxable years beginning on or after July 1, 1987. The new rates are as follows:

Taxable Income	Rate
Less than $50,000	15% of taxable income
$50,000 to $75,000	$7,500 plus 25% of the excess over $50,000
$75,000 to $100,000	$13,750 plus 34% of the excess over $75,000
$100,000 to $320,000	$22,250 plus 39% of the excess over $100,000
Above $335,000	Flat 34% on all income

For corporate taxable income in excess of $100,000, there is an additional 5% tax; that tax, though, cannot be greater than $11,000. The effect of the additional tax is to phase out the benefit of graduated rates for corporations with taxable income between $100,000 and $335,000. In effect, corporations pay a flat tax at a rate of 34% on taxable income in excess of $335,000, compared to $1,405,000 under prior law.

The old rates are as follows:

Taxable Income	Rate
Less than $25,000	15% of taxable income
$25,000 to $50,000	$3,750 plus 18% of the excess over $25,000
$50,000 to $75,000	$8,250 plus 30% of the excess over $50,000
$75,000 to $100,000	$15,750 plus 40% of the excess over $75,000
$100,000 to $1,000,000	$25,750 plus 46% of the excess over $100,000
$1,000,000 to $1,405,000	$439,750 plus 51% of the excess over $1,000,000
Above $1,405,000	Flat 46% on all income

Blending of rates. There is a blending, that is, mixing of the old and new rates for taxable years that include July 1, 1987—for instance, a taxable year that starts August 1, 1986, and ends July 30, 1987. Income received by a corporation during such a taxable year is taxed under blended rates. The rates that apply to a corporation depend on how much of its taxable year falls after July 1, 1987.

Example. Worldwide Widgets operates on a fiscal year that runs from October 1 to September 30. For the fiscal year that spans October 1, 1986 to September 30, 1987, Worldwide's taxable income is $300,000. Three-fourths of its 1986-1987 taxable year falls before July 1, 1987 (nine months of the year). Consequently, the old rates apply to three-fourths of its income and the new rates to the remaining one-fourth.

The tax on $300,000 is $117,750 under the old rates and $100,250 under the new rates. *Result:* Worldwide's tax is $113,376 for 1986-1987 (three-fourths of $117,750 plus one-fourth of $100,250).

Corporate capital gains. Under prior law, corporations received preferential treatment for their capital gains. While the top tax rate for ordinary income was 46%, long-term capital gains were taxed no higher than 28%. The Tax Reform Act eliminates this preference. Long-term gains are taxed at the same rates as ordinary income. Effective January 1, 1987, despite a higher tax on ordinary income, there is a top rate of 34% on capital gains. As under prior law, capital losses are allowable in full against capital gains.

MINIMUM TAX TIGHTENED

The alternative minimum tax (AMT) is designed to ensure that companies with substantial income cannot avoid significant tax liability through use of exclusions, deductions and credits. The 1986 Tax Reform Act replaces the prior law, add-on tax (a tax added to the regular tax) with an AMT similar to the AMT for individuals. (See chapter 2 for a discussion of the AMT for individuals.) As is true of the AMT for individuals, the AMT for corporations is paid only if it exceeds the regular income tax. The revised rules apply to taxable years beginning after 1986.

Under the new law, AMT taxable income equals (1) regular taxable income, plus (2) tax preference items, less (3) certain deductions. The AMT rate is a flat 20% applied to AMT taxable income after claiming an exemption of $40,000.

There is, though, a phase-out of the $40,000 exemption for AMT taxable income between $150,000 and $310,000. The exemption is reduced by 25% of the AMT taxable income in excess of $150,000. That translates into no exemption from AMT for a company with AMT taxable income in excess of $310,000.

Tax preference items. What follows is a listing of corporate tax preference items. In effect, these items are added back to regular tax for AMT purposes.

● **Depreciation.** The new rules apply to accelerated depreciation on all property placed in service after 1986, other than property granted a transitional exception for regular tax depreciation and investment tax credit purposes. Accelerated depreciation is a preference to the extent it exceeds alternative depreciation as computed under the new rules. For property placed in service before 1986, prior law continues to apply to corporations.

● **Pollution control facilities.** Rapid amortization of these facilities is a preference, as was true under prior law. For facilities placed in service after 1986, corporations must use the alternative recovery system.

● **Completed contract method.** Taxpayers who use the completed contract method of accounting for long-term contracts entered into after March 1, 1986, for regular income tax purposes, must use the percentage of completion method on these contracts for AMT purposes.

- **Percentage depletion.** As was true under prior law, the preference item is the difference between claimed percentage depletion and the adjusted basis of the property at the end of the year, without regard to current depletion.
- **Intangible drilling costs.** The preference item is the excess of intangible drilling costs over 65% (rather than 100%, as under prior law) of net income from oil, gas and geothermal properties for the taxable year. Excess intangible drilling costs are those expenses in excess of the amount that would have been deducted had the expenses been either deducted ratably over ten years or deducted over the life of the well as cost depletion. Net income from oil, gas and geothermal properties is gross income (excluding rent or royalties paid to another for use of the property) reduced by deductions other than excess intangible drilling costs.
- **Installment sales.** Taxpayers in the business of selling goods or real estate cannot use the installment method to defer AMT taxable income for taxable years beginning after 1986.
- **Capital gains.** They are a preference for corporations, but not for individuals.
- **Tax exempt interest on nonessential function bonds.** A new preference item is interest on most municipal bonds issued for nonessential functions after August 7, 1986.

● **Charitable contributions of appreciated property.** Another new preference item is the untaxed appreciation for a charitable contribution of property.

● **Bad debt reserves of financial institutions.** As was true under prior law, bad debt reserve addition allowances that exceed those based on an actual experience reserve are a tax preference for commercial banks and thrift institutions.

● **Shipping company capital construction funds.** Such funds are tax preferences. Deposits to the fund after 1986 are not deductible, and fund earnings after 1986 are not excludable in the determination of minimum taxable income. Pre-1987 fund deposits or earnings are treated as withdrawn before post-1986 deposits or earnings.

● **Untaxed reported profits.** One of the new items subject to AMT in 1987-1989 is an amount equal to 50% of the difference between a corporation's book income (income figures used on financial reports) and its AMT taxable income. After 1989, the use of book income to determine the amount subject to AMT will be replaced by the use of earnings and profits under revised rules for determining earnings and profits.

Other rules. Rules similar to those under the AMT for individuals apply to incentive credits, the foreign tax credit, net operating losses and the credit for minimum tax liability attributable to timing preferences. For more on these other rules, see the discussion of the AMT for individuals in chapter 2.

TIGHTER LIMIT ON BUSINESS TAX CREDITS

There is a limit on the amount of income tax liability in excess of $25,000 that can be offset by the general business credit. The new law reduces the limit from 85% to 75%. Credits now subject to the limitation include the research and development credit and the low-income housing credit.

The tighter limit applies to taxable years beginning after 1985. For a taxpayer who reports on a calendar year basis, it is the taxable year that begins on January 1, 1986.

DIVIDENDS RECEIVED DEDUCTION REDUCED

Corporations that receive certain types of dividends are allowed to take a deduction for 85% of the dividends. The new law reduces the deduction from 85% to 80%. The reduction applies to dividends received after 1986.

BASIC ALLOCATION RULES FOR ASSET ACQUISITIONS

Under the new law, both the buyer and seller in certain asset acquisitions must use a specified method to divide the purchase price among the transferred assets. The new allocation requirements retroactively apply to transactions after May 6, 1986, unless pursuant to a binding contract in effect on that date.

Under prior law, it generally was more advantageous for a seller to assign a larger portion of the purchase price to capital assets, such as goodwill. A buyer, on the other hand, preferred a higher basis for inventory or other ordinary-income assets.

Impact of new rules on sales of going concerns. The special allocation rules apply only to "applicable asset acquisitions." This term refers to any transfer of assets constituting a business in which the seller's basis is determined wholly by reference to the purchase price paid for the assets. Assets are considered to constitute a business if their character is such that goodwill or going concern value could under any circumstances attach to the assets, as, for example, when there is a distribution of a controlled corporation's stock.

Be aware that the new law covers both direct and indirect transfers of a business. So the allocation rules apply to a sale of a business by an individual or a partnership, or a sale of a partnership interest in which the basis of the purchasing partner's proportionate share of the partnership's assets is adjusted to reflect the purchase price.

Who must allocate and how. Both the buyer and seller must use what the law refers to as the residual method to allocate the purchase price among the assets acquired in the transaction. The purchase price is a key factor in figuring the buyer's basis in the assets and the seller's gain or loss on the sale. Under the residual method, the goodwill and going concern value is the excess of the business's purchase price over the aggregate fair market values of the tangible assets and the identifiable intangible assets, other than goodwill and going concern value. The method is the same as the one used in IRS administrative regulations that show how to allocate purchase price to assets following a stock purchase.

NOTE: While use of the residual method is mandatory, this does not bar an IRS challenge of the taxpayer's determination of any asset's fair market value by any appropriate method. For example, in certain cases, the IRS may reasonably make an independent showing of the value of goodwill or going concern value as a means of questioning the validity of the taxpayer's valuation of other assets.

More paperwork ahead. The new law authorizes the IRS to require the seller and buyer to file information returns disclosing amounts allocated to goodwill or going concern value, and to any other categories of assets or specific assets.

GREENMAIL PAYMENTS ARE NONDEDUCTIBLE

The new law bars a deduction by a corporation for certain types of payments made to redeem its stock. The prohibition eliminates, among other things, deduction for so-called "greenmail" payments to stockholders to avert a hostile takeover.

The new rules retroactively apply to amounts paid or incurred after February 28, 1986.

LIMITATIONS ON NET OPERATING LOSSES

Under prior law, corporations were frequently bought and sold for the net operating loss deductions that the acquired corporation could provide the acquiring corporation. The new law significantly curtails trafficking in net operating losses and other carryforwards. It does so by imposing limitations on the use of carryforwards when, as a general rule, there is a change in ownership of more than 50% of value of stock in a loss corporation, however that change is affected.

The new limitations generally apply to changes in ownership that occur after 1986. There is an exception, though, for post-1986 changes that are pursuant to tax-free reorganizations that were adopted before 1987.

EXTRAORDINARY DIVIDENDS

The new law lengthens the holding period for a reduction in basis of shares of stock held by a corporation for the untaxed part of extraordinary dividends (those that exceed 10% (5% for preferred stock) of the shareholder's basis in the stock). A corporation that sells or otherwise disposes of such shares of stock must reduce its basis if the shares have not been held for more than two years before the date of announcement or agreement about the dividend. The basis is reduced by the nontaxable portion of extraordinary dividends paid on those shares at any time during the corporation's holding period for the shares. Prior law required the basis reduction only if the shares were sold or disposed of before they had been held for one year. The revised rules apply retroactively to dividends declared after March 18, 1986.

Note, though, that the basis reduction is required only to determine gain or loss on the disposition of the shares. If the aggregate nontaxed portions of extraordinary dividends exceed the shareholder's basis, the excess is treated as gain from a sale or exchange at the time of disposition.

Special option. The revised rules give taxpayers an option that is advantageous when the shares have appreciated significantly since their original purchase. Taxpayers can determine the distribution's status as an extraordinary dividend by reference to the fair market value of the shares on the day before the ex-dividend date, instead of the adjusted basis. Fair market value, however, must be acceptable to the IRS.

No double reduction. The law bars using any portion of a distribution to reduce basis twice, as when the corporate shareholder and the payor of the dividend are members of an affiliated group that file consolidated returns.

COMPUTER SOFTWARE ROYALTIES

The law authorizes a new exemption for royalties received by computer software developers from the penalty tax on personal holding companies. The exemption is available for qualifying companies that are actively engaged in the business of developing computer software. The exemption retroactively applies to all taxable years, except for years closed for refund applications by the statute of limitations.

UTILITIES USING ACCRUAL ACCOUNTING

Utilities using the accrual method of accounting are subject to a new rule for taxable years beginning after 1986. They must recognize earned but unbilled income not later than the year in which they provide service to customers.

TITLE HOLDING COMPANIES

The law creates a new type of tax-exempt status for title holding companies. To qualify for the exemption, a title holding company cannot have more than 35 related or unrelated tax-exempt organizations as shareholders or beneficiaries and must meet other specified requirements. These rules apply to taxable years beginning after 1986.

12
BUSINESS TAXES

NEW RULES FOR DEPRECIATION DEDUCTIONS

Meaning of depreciation. Depreciation is an expense deduction that allows you to charge off, that is, recover or write off, your capital investments in equipment, machines, fixtures, autos, trucks and buildings used in your business, profession or rental or other income-producing activities. No depreciation, though, may be claimed on property held for personal purposes, such as a personal residence or pleasure car. When a car or other property is used for both business and pleasure, only the business portion may be depreciated.

Depreciation is deducted annually. Even though the deduction may give you no tax benefit in a particular year because your other deductions already exceed your income, you may not choose to forego the depreciation deduction and, instead, accumulate it for high income years. Similarly, incorrect deductions claimed in prior years may not be corrected by an adjustment to your present depreciation deduction. If the year in which the error was made is not yet closed by the statute of limitations, you may file an amended return to adjust the depreciation deduction for that year.

Investment credit repealed. The Tax Reform Act repeals the investment credit for property placed in service after 1985, except for assets contracted for before 1986 but placed in service at certain dates in 1986.

New depreciation system. The new law retains much of the simplicity and fast writeoffs of the accelerated cost recovery system (ACRS), which allows rapid depreciation for most items and eliminates disputes over useful life, salvage value and depreciation methods. But the tax legislation lengthens the depreciation period for real estate, which is the big loser under the revised ACRS setup and is discussed below. The modifications made to the ACRS structure by the Tax Reform Act are generally effective for property placed in service after December 31, 1986. But you can elect to use either the old or the new depreciation rules for property placed in service after July 31, 1986 and before December 31, 1986.

Equipment purchases. Under the new rules, there is a five-year recovery period for some equipment purchases. Items in this category include cars, which are discussed below, light trucks, computers and typewriters. For most other equipment, including office furniture and fixtures, the recovery period is seven years.

First-year expensing. Under the rules applicable to a return for 1986, you can elect to take an immediate, year-of-acquisition deduction for up to $5,000 of the cost of business equipment, instead of depreciating the cost under ACRS rules. The Tax Reform Act raises to $10,000 ($5,000 for a married person filing separately) the amount of equipment that you can expense in a year, starting with 1987. The expensing deduction cannot, however, be used by large purchasers. If you buy more than $200,000 of eligible property during a year, the expensing deduction ceiling is reduced on a dollar-for-dollar basis for purchases in excess of $200,000.

NOTE: You cannot claim depreciation deductions on the portion of equipment purchases that you expense. But since the investment tax credit is eliminated as of January 1, 1986, you no longer forfeit a tax credit when you elect to expense equipment purchases.

Business cars. The rules applicable to a return for 1986 allow taxpayers to write off the cost of business cars over three years—25% of the cost the first year, 38% the second year, and 37% the third year. But the Tax Reform Act changes this for cars placed in service after 1986. The revised rules categorize cars as five-year writeoff property. Actually, it takes six years to write off the cost of a car. Reason: Under the new law, your depreciation deductions start on July 1 of the year you place the car in service, so the five-year writeoff period runs over into a sixth calendar year.

Despite the longer depreciation periods, you will suffer only a small cut in your annual writeoffs—at least in the early years. This is because the new law accelerates the rate at which you write off your cost. For example, under the old rules, you could deduct 63% of your cost in the first two years; under the new rules, it's 52%.

Prior law authorized use of the accelerated method of computing deductions only if you used your car more than 50% for business. Otherwise, the car had to be written off through straight-line depreciation. Moreover, there was a cap on depreciation deductions for cars costing over $12,800. Your depreciation deductions for a business car could not exceed $3,200 for the first year and $4,800 for subsequent years. (These figures were reduced proportionately for cars used only partially for business.)

The new law leaves the 50% business use rule intact. And depreciation deductions for cars costing more than $12,800 continue to be subject to depreciation caps. However, the yearly amount of the caps is reduced to reflect the new, slightly less favorable depreciation schedule.

The maximum depreciation deduction is $2,560 for the first year, $4,100 for the second year, $2,450 for the third year and $1,475 for each succeeding year. Of course, these reduced deduction limits produce even smaller tax savings in the new lower tax brackets.

Tax strategy. If you are planning to buy a business car in the next several months, try to place it in service before the end of 1986. Then seek to maximize your percentage of business use for 1986.

If you put the car in service in late December, 1986, and use it only for business, you are entitled to a 1986 depreciation deduction of 25% of the car's cost (subject to a $3,200 deduction ceiling). You keep this big writeoff even if your business use percentage drops below 100% in subsequent years (as long as it does not drop to 50% or less). And you lock in the present three-year depreciation schedule for computing your 1987 and 1988 deductions.

Real estate. For properties placed in service after 1986, the Tax Reform Act both lengthens the depreciation period and changes the rate at which the properties can be written off. Under prior rules, both commercial and residential rental real estate were depreciable over 19 years. Real estate could also be written off at a rate that produced bigger deductions in the early years of ownership than in the later years. The new law increases the depreciation period to 27½ years for residential rental property and 31½ years for commercial property. And both types must be written off using slower straight-line depreciation.

Tax strategy. If you are looking to buy some rental real estate, buy it this year so you can use the 19-year ACRS tables. But a word of caution: To the extent you feel that property values on rental property will decline (for example, due to the restrictions on tax shelter losses that are discussed in chapter 7 and the tougher depreciation schedules), you may want to wait until next year.

FINANCE LEASING REPEALED

The new law repeals the finance leasing rules for agreements entered into after 1986, except for property that qualifies for finance lease transition rules under legislation enacted prior to the Tax Reform Act of 1986.

TARGETED JOBS CREDIT EXTENDED

The targeted jobs credit is designed to encourage business employment of the hard-to-hire. The credit is based on a percentage of wages.

The Tax Reform Act extends the credit for three additional years. But the Act reduces from 50% to 40% the credit for the first $6,000 of first-year wages of eligible individuals. The 40% credit applies to wages paid individuals who begin work before 1989.

The new law repeals the credit of 25% of the first $6,000 of second-year wages. Also, wages do not count for credit purposes unless an individual is (1) employed by the employer for at least 90 days (14 days for economically disadvantaged summer youth employees) or (2) completes at least 120 hours (20 for summer employees).

These changes apply to individuals who begin work after 1985 and before 1989.

BUSINESS ENERGY CREDITS EXTENDED

The Tax Reform Act allows businesses to claim energy credits ranging from 10% to 15% for specified taxable years for the following types of property:

Property	Credit Percentage	From	To
Solar energy	15%	1-1-86	12-31-86
	12%	1-1-87	12-31-87
	10%	1-1-88	12-31-88
Geothermal	15%	1-1-86	12-31-86
	10%	1-1-87	12-31-88
Ocean Thermal	15%	1-1-86	12-31-88
Biomass	15%	1-1-86	12-31-86
	10%	1-1-87	12-31-87

Under prior law, all of these credits were supposed to expire at the end of 1985. Previously, the biomass credit was 10%. The Tax Reform Act allows the business credits for wind energy property, inter city busses and small hydroelectric projects, and the individual residential energy credit to expire at the end of 1985.

RESEARCH AND DEVELOPMENT CREDIT EXTENDED

The 1986 Tax Act revives and modifies the credit for research and development. The new law grants a three-year lease on life to the credit, which had expired at the end of 1985. It reduces the credit from 25% to 20% and modifies the definition of eligible expenditures to encourage research that is undertaken to discover information that is technological in nature and that is intended to result in a new item for sale or use by the taxpayer in its business.

CAPITALIZING INVENTORY, CONSTRUCTION AND DEVELOPMENT COSTS

Uniform capitalization rules. The 1986 Act changes the rules for capitalization of costs incurred to produce, acquire and hold property. Under the new law, uniform rules for determining costs that must be capitalized, rather than be deducted currently, generally apply to all manufacturers, retailers and wholesalers that produce property or acquire property for resale. The uniform rules, therefore, apply to inventory, noninventory property held for sale to customers and assets constructed for self-use. These rules are subject to an exception for wholesalers and retailers with gross receipts of $10,000,000 or less.

In general, the new rules apply to costs paid or incurred after 1986. In the case of inventories, they apply to the taxpayer's first taxable year beginning after 1986.

Interest. A special rule requires capitalization of interest only for real or personal property produced by the taxpayer that has: (1) a long useful life; (2) an estimated production period of more than two years; or (3) an estimated production period of more than one year and a cost of more than $1,000,000. This rule applies to interest incurred after 1986.

Long-term contracts. In general, all long-term contracts are subject to the uniform capitalization rules. Also treated as contract costs are general and administrative expenses identified under the contract or Federal certification procedures as contract-related. This rule applies to contracts entered into after Feburary 28, 1986.

TRADEMARK AND TRADE NAME AMORTIZATION REPEALED

The new law repeals the election to amortize, over a period of at least 60 months, expenditures for acquiring, protecting, expanding, registering or defending a trademark or trade name. Consequently, trademarks and trade name expenditures must be capitalized and generally recovered on disposition of the asset.

The repeal applies to expenditures paid or incurred after 1986. However, prior law remains applicable to certain expenditures. They are expenditures incurred (1) pursuant to a written contract that was binding as of March 1, 1986; or (2) as to developing, protecting, expanding, registering or defending trademarks or trade names begun as of March 1, 1986, if the lesser of $1 million or 5% of the cost has been incurred or committed by that date. In each case, though, the trademark or trade name must be placed in service before 1988.

REMOVAL OF ARCHITECTURAL BARRIERS TO THE HANDICAPPED AND ELDERLY

The new law makes permanent the provision allowing immediate expensing of up to $35,000 for costs incurred to remove architectural and transportation barriers to the handicapped and elderly. Previously, this break was available only for expenses incurred in taxable years beginning before 1986.

RESTRICTIONS ON USE OF CASH BASIS METHOD

Under the cash basis method, a taxpayer generally reports income when actually or constructively received and deducts expenses in the taxable year in which they are paid. The Tax Reform Act imposes restrictions on use of the cash method. These restrictions apply, as a general rule, to taxable years that begin after 1986. For a taxpayer who reports on a calendar year basis, it is the taxable year that starts on January 1, 1987.

The key restriction is that the cash method cannot be used by a C corporation (the kind that is taxed at the corporate level, as opposed to an S corporation that is taxed at the shareholder level), a partnership that has a C corporation as a partner or a tax shelter. In general, the cash method can continue to be used by individuals, farmers, personal service corporations (professional corporations formed by doctors, lawyers and the like) and entities (other than tax shelters) with average annual gross receipts of less than $5,000,000 for the three preceding taxable years.

USE OF INSTALLMENT SALE REPORTING RESTRICTED

In general, installment sale reporting is available for a sale of property when one or more payments will be received in a later year or years. The seller is taxed as payments are received, rather than being taxed on the entire gain in the year of sale. The 1986 Tax Reform Act, however, places several restrictions on use of the installment method to report sales of property.

Outstanding debt limitations. First, the new law limits installment reporting under a formula generally based on the ratio of the taxpayer's debt to assets. The limitation applies to (1) all sales of property held for sale to customers, that is, inventory-type items, and (2) sales of business or rental property (other than certain farm property) when the selling price of such property exceeds $150,000. Note, though, that this limitation does not apply to personal use property and certain farm property and debt related to such property.

A special rule applies to taxpayers who sell certain unimproved residential lots and timeshares (a timeshare is the right to use a specified parcel of residential real property, including campground sites, for up to six weeks a year). These sellers can elect to pay interest on the deferred tax liability attributable to use of the installment method, rather than be subject to the ratio-of-debts-to assets-limitations under the new law.

Another special rule applies to manufacturer/dealer sales of tangible personal property. There is an exception from the new limitations when (1) the dealer has to make principal payments to the manufacturer only when the dealer resells or rents the property; (2) the manufacturer has the right to repurchase the property at a fixed or ascertainable price within nine months of the sale to the dealer; and (3) certain other conditions are met.

The ratio-of-debts-to-assets limitations apply as of January 1, 1987, for sales on or after March 1, 1986.

Revolving credit plans. Second, the new law bars installment reporting for sales under revolving credit plans. This restriction applies to sales after 1986.

Publicly traded property. Third, the new law bars installment reporting for sales of stocks, bonds and other property sold on the New York, American and other established securities exchanges.

Under the new rules, gains must be recognized on the trade date, instead of the settlement date as allowed by prior law.

This change affects investors who realize gains on stocks sold during the final trading days of one year, but do not receive payment until the next year. Previous law permitted a choice for sellers. They were not taxed until the payment year, unless they elected not to use installment reporting and to be taxed in the sale year.

This restriction applies to sales of publicly traded property after 1986.

TAXABLE YEAR OF PARTNERSHIPS, S CORPORATIONS AND PERSONAL SERVICE CORPORATIONS

The new law ends a tax deferral strategy for partners and for shareholders of certain kinds of closely held businesses. The crackdown takes the form of a requirement that applies to partnerships, S corporations (the type of corporation that is taxed in a manner similar to a partnership in that tax ordinarily imposed is on the shareholders of the S corporation, rather than on the corporation itself) and personal service corporations (professional service corporations formed by doctors, lawyers and the like who are employee-owners). Partnerships, S corporations and personal service corporations must use taxable years that generally conform to the taxable years of their owners. This change applies to taxable years beginning after 1986.

To illustrate the previously available strategy, assume that AB partnership uses a taxable year that ends on January 31, while its partners, Anderson and Benson, report their income on a calendar year basis. Anderson and Benson are not taxed on AB's income until the end of its taxable year. Consequently, Anderson and Benson are able to defer taxes on eleven months of business profits as AB's earnings from February through December are not treated as income to the two partners until the following year.

Here's another variation of the no longer available maneuver. A doctor reports income on a calendar year and is the employee-owner of a professional corporation with a taxable year that ends on January 31. The doctor earns $200,000 a year, but receives a salary of $10,000 each month, or $120,000 for the year. Then, in January of the next year, the remaining $80,000 goes to the doctor as a bonus. *Result:* The entire $200,000 of compensation is deductible by the fiscal-year corporation in one taxable year. The calendar-year doctor, though, reports the $200,000 over two taxable years. No deferral is allowed for the salary of $120,000; those earnings are reportable in the first year. But the January bonus of $80,000 does not become reportable until the following year.

These tax deferral techniques are prohibited by the new rules. Now, a partnership has to have the same taxable year as that of its partners owing a majority interest in partnership profits and capital. If the majority owners do not have the same taxable year, the partnership must adopt the same taxable year as its principal partners. If the principal partners do not have the same taxable year, and no majority of its partners have the same taxable year, the partnership must adopt a calendar year as its taxable year.

As for an S corporation, it must adopt a permitted year, regardless of when it elected S status.

A personal service corporation must adopt a calendar year. Also, a personal service corporation cannot deduct payments to owner-employees before the year paid.

Exception. The new rules are subject to a limited exception. Where the partnership, S corporation or personal service corporation satisfies the IRS that there is a business purpose (such as a natural business year) for having a different taxable year, such different year is permissible, provided deferral is three months or less.

A partnership need not adopt the tax year of its majority interest partners unless partners having the same taxable year have owned a majority interest in partnership profits and capital for the partnership's preceding three taxable years.

Change of taxable year. A business affected by the revised rules will have two taxable years in 1987—the first one under the old system that ends during the year (on January 31, say) and the second one that ends on December 31, as required by the new law.

A partnership, S corporation or personal service corporation that is required to change its taxable year is treated as doing so with the IRS's consent. For a partnership or S corporation, each partner or owner may elect to take the excess of income over expenses for a short taxable year (a taxable year of less than 12 months) resulting from the change into income ratably over the first four taxable years (including the owner's year which would otherwise include the income or loss of the entity's short taxable year) beginning after 1986. Without an election, net income or loss for the short taxable year is included currently in its entirety. The short taxable year of a personal service corporation that results from the change of taxable year is annualized.

BAD DEBT RESERVES

The new law generally repeals the reserve method of deducting bad debts for taxpayers other than banks with assets of less than $500,000,000 and all thrift institutions. Also repealed is the reserve method for dealers who guarantee, endorse or provide indemnity agreements for debts owed to others. To be allowed as a deduction for income tax purposes, wholly worthless business debts need not be treated as worthless on a taxpayer's books.

These changes apply to taxable years beginning after 1986. For a taxpayer who reports income on a calendar year basis, it is the taxable year that begins on January 1, 1987.

QUALIFIED DISCOUNT COUPONS

The new law repeals the election that allows taxpayers who issue qualified discount coupons (coupons that are issued and redeemable by the taxpayer and allow consumers discounts on the purchase price of merchandise or other tangible personal property) to take a current-year deduction for redemption costs, even though some coupons may actually be redeemed the following year. Under the new rules, a current deduction is allowed only for redemption costs of coupons that have been received by the close of the taxable year. The change applies to taxable years beginning after 1986.

SOLVENT DEBTOR'S DISCHARGED BUSINESS DEBT

The new law repeals the prior law exclusion from income for the discharge, that is, the cancellation or forgiveness of a qualified business indebtedness. This change applies to debt discharges occurring after 1986.

The effect of this change is to require the current reporting of income from a debt discharge, unless the discharge occurs in a bankruptcy case or the debtor is insolvent. Congress wanted to eliminate what it referred to as the "disparate treatment" under prior law when the full benefit of the deferral was unavailable for a taxpayer who did not have sufficient amounts of inventory or depreciable assets.

INTANGIBLE DRILLING COSTS

The Tax Reform Act increases, from 20% to 30%, the amount of otherwise deductible intangible drilling costs that integrated producer corporations must capitalize and amortize. Also, the Act increases the amortization period from 36 months to five years. These charges apply to costs paid or incurred after 1986.

FOREIGN INTANGIBLE DRILLING AND MINING EXPLORATION

The new law authorizes similar treatment for intangible drilling and development costs and mining exploration and development costs incurred outside of the United States. Under the revised rules, these costs are recovered (1) over a 10-year, straight line amortization schedule, beginning in the year they are paid or incurred or (2) at the taxpayer's election, by adding them to the basis for cost depletion. The revised rules generally apply to costs paid or incurred after 1986.

SOIL AND WATER CONSERVATION DEDUCTIONS RESTRICTED

Farmers have the option to currently deduct certain capital expenses, such as soil and water conservation costs. The new law limits the deduction for these costs. They are deductible only if for improvements that are consistent with a conservation plan approved by the Department of Agriculture's Soil Conservation Service. If no SCS plan exists for the location, improvement costs that are consistent with a plan of a State conservation agency are deemed to satisfy the Federal standards.

Under the new rules, there are no soil-and-water deductions for these costs:

- Draining;
- Filling of wetlands; and
- Operating a center pivot irrigation system.

The new rules apply to costs incurred after 1985.

DEDUCTION FOR LAND CLEARING COSTS REPEALED

The new law ends the option available to farmers to currently deduct land clearing costs. Now they must be added to the land's basis, in the case of costs incurred after 1986.

NOTE: Congressional committee reports state that routine brush clearing and other ordinary maintenance activities related to property already used in farming continue to be currently deductible to the extent they qualify as ordinary and necessary business expenses, rather than capital expenditures.

TOUGHER RULES FOR DISPOSITIONS OF CONVERTED WETLANDS

The new law bars capital gain treatment for gains on the disposition of converted wetlands or highly erodible croplands that are converted to agricultural uses (other than livestock grazing). These gains are treated as ordinary income. Also, losses on such dispositions are long-term capital losses, not ordinary income. These changes apply to dispositions of land converted after March 1, 1986.

Key definitions. "Converted wetlands" means land (1) that is converted wetland within the meaning of the 1985 Food Security Act, and (2) that is held by the person who originally converted the wetland, by a person who uses the land for farming for any period following the conversion, or by a person whose adjusted basis in the property is determined by reference to the basis of the person in whose hands the property was converted. Land that had been converted could become eligible for capital gain treatment in the hands of a later buyer or legatee, provided the buyer or legatee has used the land only for nonfarming purposes.

Generally, the Food Security Act defines converted wetland as land that has been drained or filled for the purpose of making the production of agricultural goods possible, if the production would not have been possible but for this action.

"Highly erodible cropland" means any land as defined in the Food Security Act that the taxpayer uses for farming other than animal grazing. Generally, highly erodible cropland is land that (1) the Department of Agriculture classifies as class IV, VI, VII or VIII land under its land capability classification system, or (2) that would have an excess average annual rate of erosion in relation to the soil loss tolerance level, as determined by the Secretary of Agriculture.

PREPAYMENT OF FARMING EXPENSES

The Tax Reform Act stops cash basis farmers from deducting specified amounts paid for feed, seed, fertilizer and other similar farm supplies earlier than the time when the feed, seed, fertilizer or other supplies are actually used or consumed. That means no deduction until the tax year in which economic performance occurs.

Farming defined. Farming means, generally, the cultivation of land or the raising of any agricultural or horticultural commodity, including animals.

Who is subject to the new restriction? Generally, it applies to any farmer to the extent that more than 50% of the person's farming expenses paid during the tax year (other than prepaid farm supplies) are prepaid expenses. The new law does not, however, treat such taxpayers as farm syndicates. For purposes of the 50% test, expenses include farm operating expenses, such as ordinary and necessary farming expenses, interest and taxes paid, depreciation allowances on farm equipment and other expenses generally reported on Schedule F of Form 1040.

Exceptions. The 50% test is subject to two exceptions. If either of the exceptions are met, prepaid expenses remain deductible as allowed by prior law. This holds true even though the prepaid expenses are more than 50% of farming expenses for that year.

The first exception applies if an "eligible farmer," as defined below, fails to satisfy the 50% test due to a change in business operations directly attributable to extraordinary circumstances, including government crop diversion programs.

The second exception applies if the eligible farmer satisfies the 50% test on the basis of the three preceding taxable years. For this purpose, the expenses for the three-year period are aggregated.

"Eligible farmer" defined. The term includes: (1) any person whose principal, that is, year-round, residence is on the farm; (2) any person with a principal occupation of farming; or (3) any family member of persons described in (1) or (2).

The exception applies only to an eligible farmer's farming activities attributable to the farm on which the residence is located, or to farms included in the "principal occupation" of farming activities.

When the new rules become applicable. They apply to amounts with respect to which a deduction would be allowable under prior law after March 1, 1986.

REPLANTING LAND DESTROYED BY FREEZING

The new law authorizes a special deduction rule for planting and maintenance costs incurred following loss or damage to a grove, orchard or vineyard as a result of freezing temperatures, disease, drought, pests or casualty. These costs can be deducted by persons other than the farmer who owned the grove, orchard or vineyard at the time of the damage. Also, replanting need not take place on the same property. Therefore, costs incurred at a different location (although not exceeding the original acreage), but by the same taxpayer, can qualify. To come under the new rules, two conditions have to be met.

First, the taxpayer who owned the property at the time of the loss or damage must have an equity interest of more than 50% in the property. Second, the additional persons incurring the loss must hold part of the remaining equity interest in the property and must materially participate in the planting, cultivation, maintenance or development.

The new rules apply to costs paid or incurred after the date that President Reagan signed the 1986 Tax Reform Act.

DISCHARGE FROM FARM DEBT

To help alleviate the credit crisis for farmers, the new law revises the rules for discharge from farm debt.

Under the new rules, discharge of indebtedness income arising from an agreement between a solvent individual engaged in the business of farming and an unrelated person to discharge qualified farming indebtedness is treated as income realized by an insolvent individual.

Generally, if an insolvent taxpayer receives income from discharge of business indebtedness, the taxpayer can exclude that income if the taxpayer's "tax attributes" are reduced by the amount of the income. Tax attributes include otherwise unused net operating loss deductions, investment tax credits, foreign tax credits, capital loss carryovers and basis of the taxpayer's depreciable property. If the amount of discharge of indebtedness income exceeds the taxpayer's available tax attributes, tax on the excess income is forgiven to the extent of the taxpayer's insolvency.

Qualified agricultural indebtedness is a debt incurred to finance producing agricultural products (including timber) or livestock in the United States, or farm business debt secured by farmland or farm machinery and equipment used in agricultural production.

Individuals are treated as engaged in farming if at least 50% of the average annual gross receipts during the three taxable years preceding the year in which the discharge of indebtedness occurs were derived from farming.

Also, the new law includes basis in farmland in the list of tax attributes that may be reduced by the discharge of indebtedness income. However, all tax attributes other than basis in farmland, including property other than farmland, must be reduced before the discharge of indebtedness income is applied against that attribute.

The new rules apply to discharge of indebtedness income realized after April 9, 1986.

DEPRECIATION RECAPTURE ON INSTALLMENT SALES OF IRRIGATION EQUIPMENT

The bill passed by the Senate included a special rule for depreciation recapture income resulting from an installment sale of equipment used to irrigate farmland. The Senate proposal would have authorized the income to be reported under the installment method, rather than, as under existing law, entirely in the year of sale. This proposal was dropped from the final version of the Tax Reform Act.

CO-OP APARTMENTS

The law authorizes pass-through treatment for owners of co-op apartments. An owner (the law refers to the owner as a tenant-stockholder who owns shares of stock that entitle him to occupy a particular apartment in the co-op building) can deduct his share of payments made by the co-op corporation for mortgage interest and real estate taxes.

But pass-through treatment is available only if, among other things, the co-op derives at least 80% of its gross income from tenant-stockholders. Under prior law, as a general rule, only individuals can be tenant-stockholders. The Tax Reform Act makes pass-through treatment available to corporations, estates and other entities, not just to individuals.

The Act also limits a tenant-stockholder's depreciation deduction to his basis for the stock. A deduction in excess of basis can be carried forward to later years.

Under the new law, there is no deduction for payments that are properly chargeable to the co-op's capital account. A disallowed deduction, however, does not vanish. It increases a tenant-stockholder's adjusted basis for his stock, thereby decreasing gain or increasing loss on a later sale or other transfer.

The revised rules apply to taxable years that begin after 1986.

BUS OPERATING AUTHORITIES

The new law allows owners of certain bus operating authorities an ordinary deduction ratably over five years for loss in value of such authorities. This rule applies retroactively to taxable years ending after November 18, 1982.

BAD DEBT RESERVES FOR THRIFT INSTITUTIONS

The new law reduces from 40% to 8% the maximum percentage of income that can be deducted as an addition to the reserve for bad debts by a thrift institution (a mutual savings bank, domestic building and loan association or a cooperative bank). This change applies to taxable years beginning after 1986.

EXEMPTION FROM UNRELATED BUSINESS INCOME TAX

The new law authorizes an exemption from the unrelated business income tax in the case of rentals of membership lists of tax-exempt organizations. This rule applies to transactions occurring after the date President Reagan signed the 1986 Tax Reform Act.

13
FILING TAX RETURNS AND TAX AUDITS

WITHHOLDING CHANGES

Congress has told the IRS to make changes in the W-4 Form that employees use to claim withholding exemptions and in the withholding tables that employers use to determine how much to take out for taxes. Reason for the changes? To have the amount withheld from an employee's wages more closely match the employee's actual tax liability under the amendments made by the Tax Reform Act.

All employees must file revised W-4 Forms by September 30, 1987. If an employee fails to do so, an employer must withhold income taxes as if the employee claimed one allowance (if the employer checked the "Single" box on the most recent W-4 that the employee filed) or two allowances (if the employee checked the "Married" box).

HIGHER ESTIMATED TAX PAYMENTS FOR INDIVIDUALS

Income taxes are collected on a pay-as-you-go basis through withholding on wages and pensions, as well as estimated tax payments on other income. Where all or most of your income is from wages, pensions and annuities, you generally do not have to pay estimated tax because your estimated tax liability has been satisfied by withholding. But do not assume that you are not required to pay simply because taxes have been withheld from your wages. Always check your estimated tax liability. Withholding may not cover your tax; the withholding tax rate may be below your actual tax rate when considering other income, such as interest, dividends, business income and gains from sales of investments.

Failure to pay or an underpayment of estimated tax may subject you to a penalty. You do not, however, have to make estimated tax payments if your estimated tax is less than $500.

The Tax Reform Act increases from 80% to 90% the proportion of the current year's tax liability that you must make as estimated payments to avoid the penalty. Under the new law, quarterly estimated installments must be 22.5%, 45%, 67.5% and 90% of the year's liability, up from the previous 20%, 40%, 60% and 80%.

The new rules apply starting with returns for 1987 to be filed in 1988. Therefore, the 80% rule remains applicable to the estimated payment due January 15, 1987, which is the final payment for 1986. All subsequent estimated payments are, however, subject to the 90% rule.

NOTE: The Tax Reform Act left unchanged the easiest way to avoid the penalty if your estimated payments are less than 80% for 1986 or 90% for 1987. To sidestep a penalty for, say, 1986, all you need to do is figure and pay as your estimated tax an amount equal to or more than the tax shown on your 1985 tax return. Include the 1985 self-employment tax if you are self-employed. Also include estimated liability for alternative minimum tax, which is discussed at chapter 2. To qualify for this exception to the penalty, you must have filed a 1985 return covering a period of 12 months.

WAIVER OF ESTIMATED PAYMENT PENALTIES

Some of the changes made by the Tax Reform Act increase tax liabilities from the start of 1986.

Consequently, the act allows individuals until April 15, 1987 and corporations until March 15, 1987, to pay their full 1986 tax liabilities without incurring penalties for underpayments of estimated taxes. The penalty relief, however, applies only to underpayments attributable to changes made by the act.

ESTIMATED PAYMENTS BY TRUSTS AND ESTATES

Prior law did not require trusts and estates to make estimated income tax payments. Trusts had to pay their income taxes by the due date for filing a return. As for estates, they could pay their income taxes in four equal installments, beginning with the due date for a return and for each three month period thereafter.

The Tax Reform Act requires both new and existing trusts and estates to pay estimated taxes in the same manner as individuals. (The rules for individuals are discussed in the first section of this chapter.) An estate, however, need not make estimated payments in its first two years. The Act also repeals the rules that allowed estates to pay their income tax over four equal installments.

The new requirements apply to taxable years beginning after 1986.

NEW METHOD OF CALCULATING INTEREST RATES ON DEFICIENCIES AND REFUNDS

Under prior law, both taxpayers and the IRS pay interest on underpayments and overpayments at the same rate—the prime rate charged by large commercial banks. The Tax Reform Act sets different rates for underpayments and overpayments.

The new rules peg the overpayment rate as the Federal short-term rate plus two percentage points. The underpayment rate is one percentage point higher than the overpayment rate, that is, three percentage points above the Federal short-term rate. Both are to be rounded to the nearest full percentage.

The rate is adjusted quarterly, is determined during the first month of each quarter and takes effect the following quarter. For example, the Federal short-term rate for January is the rate used to determine the interest to be charged on underpayments and overpayments for April, May and June.

The IRS determines the interest rate based on average market yield on outstanding U.S. marketable obligations with remaining maturity periods of three years or less.

The new rules apply to interest for periods after 1986.

INTEREST RATE ON TAX SHELTER DEFICIENCIES

The law authorizes the IRS to charge interest on tax shelter deficiencies at a higher rate than the regular rate. The higher rate applies when, for any taxable year, there is a deficiency of more than $1,000 that is attributable to a tax-motivated transaction, such as a tax shelter. The rate on a shelter deficiency is 120% of the regular rate.

Under the Tax Reform Act, the 120% rate also applies to sham or fraudulent transactions. The revised rule applies to interest that accrues after 1984.

INTEREST ON ACCUMULATED EARNINGS TAX

The law imposes an accumulated earnings tax to penalize corporations (the closely held type, in most cases) that accumulate, rather than distribute, income, so as to reduce or avoid taxes. Under prior law, interest was charged only from the date the IRS demanded payment of the tax, rather than the date the return was originally due to be filed. The Tax Reform Act imposes interest on accumulated earnings tax underpayments from the return due date.

The new rules apply to returns with due dates (without considering filing extensions) after 1985.

ABATEMENTS OF INTEREST

IRS errors or delays sometimes cause taxpayers to incur additional interest charges. This may even occur after the underlying tax liability has been correctly adjusted by the IRS or admitted by the taxpayer. According to Congressional committee reports, where an IRS official acting in his official capacity fails to perform a ministerial act, which is legalese for a routine administrative act, such as issuing either a statutory notice of deficiency or notice and demand for payment after all procedural and substantive preliminaries have been completed, the IRS should have the authority to abate the interest independent of the underlying tax liability.

To supply the IRS with such authority, the new law says that the IRS can abate interest that is generated because an IRS official either fails to perform an administrative act in a timely fashion or errs in performing an administrative act, provided the taxpayer is not at least partially responsible for the delay. Although the IRS is authorized to abate interest, it is not required to do so, except in cases of erroneous refunds of less than $50,000.

Congress does not want the IRS to routinely use the provision. It is to be used in cases where failure to abate would be grossly unfair. Also, interest is to be abated only for the time attributable to the failure to perform the administrative act that occurs after the IRS contacts the taxpayer. Only those acts occurring after preliminary prerequisites, such as conferencing and supervisory review, are to be considered administrative acts for this purpose.

Example. If there is an unreasonable delay in issuing a 90-day letter (deficiency notice) after the IRS and the taxpayer have completed efforts to resolve the matter, that provides grounds for an interest abatement.

Congress has authorized the IRS to issue regulations that explain what constitutes reasonable delay.

Generally, the IRS cannot charge interest on money that a taxpayer owes because of an IRS error. For instance, a taxpayer who gets a $1,000 refund, rather than the $100 refund he is entitled to, because of an IRS error, will not be charged interest on the excess $900. But there are two exceptions to the no-interest-on-refund rule. The IRS can charge interest on an erroneous excess refund when either:

(1) the taxpayer has caused the overstated refund to occur; or (2) the erroneous refund exceeds $50,000.

The new rules apply to interest accruing in taxable years that begin after 1978.

SUSPENSION OF INTEREST COMPOUNDING

The new law suspends both the interest on a tax deficiency and the compounded interest on the previously accrued interest. The suspension starts 31 days after the taxpayer has filed a waiver of restrictions on assessment of the underlying taxes and ends when a notice and demand is issued to the taxpayer.

The new rule applies to interest accruing after 1982.

INCREASED PENALTY FOR FAILURE TO PAY

The new law increases the penalty for failure to pay taxes from .5% (¹/₂ of 1%) to 1%. The increased rate applies after the IRS notifies the taxpayer of its intention to levy on the assets of the taxpayer.

Relief for penalty overlap eliminated. The failure to pay penalty can no longer be reduced by the failure to file penalty.

When the new rules apply. They apply to assessments after 1986.

NEGLIGENCE AND FRAUD PENALTIES

Negligence penalties. The penalty for negligent or intentional disregard of IRS rules now applies to all taxes under the Internal Revenue Code. The penalty rate remains 5%, and continues to apply to the entire underpayment, not just to the portion of an underpayment that is attributable to negligence.

NOTE. A taxpayer who fails to report on a tax return any kind of income listed on a Form 1099 information return (not just interest and dividend payments, as under prior law) is automatically considered to be negligent, unless there is clear and convincing evidence to the contrary.

Fraud penalties. The penalty rate increases from 50% to 75%.

NOTE: Under the new rules, the penalty applies only to the portion of an underpayment that is actually attributable to fraud. Before, if there was an underpayment of $1,000,000 and even $1 of it was attributable to fraud, the *entire* underpayment was subject to the penalty. Now, though, when the IRS finds fraud, the taxpayer has the burden of showing what part of the underpayment is not attributable to fraud. If the taxpayer is able to do so, that part of the underpayment escapes the fraud penalty.

When the new rules apply. They apply to returns that have due dates (without regard to filing extensions) after 1986.

INFORMATION RETURN PENALTIES

The IRS can exact penalties from payers of dividends and other kinds of income for their failure to file Form 1099 information returns with the IRS, as well as for their failure to supply copies of those 1099 Forms to the income recipients. The Tax Reform Act consolidates those penalties and increases the maximum penalty from $50,000 to $100,000.

The Act also establishes a new penalty for failure to include correct information on 1099 Forms. The maximum penalty is $20,000.

The new rules apply to 1099 Forms with due dates (without regard to filing extensions) after 1986.

INCREASED PENALTY FOR SUBSTANTIAL UNDERPAYMENT OF TAX

The new law increases the penalty for a substantial underpayment of tax from 10% to 20% of the underpayment. An underpayment is substantial when it exceeds the greater of $5,000 ($10,000 for most corporations) or 10% of the proper tax. The increased penalty applies to returns with due dates (without regard to filing extensions) after 1986.

TAX SHELTER REGISTRATION

Tax shelter organizers must register certain shelters with the IRS. Prior law required registration when, among other things, the shelter ratio (the ratio of deductions and 200% of the credits to cash actually invested) was greater than two to one. The new law substitutes 300% for 200% in determining the ratio, starting with shelter sales after 1986.

The IRS can exact a penalty from a shelter that fails to register. The new law increases the minimum penalty for failure to register. Previously, it was the greater of $500 or 1% of the aggregate amount invested in the shelter, up to a maximum of $10,000. Now, it is the greater of $500 or 1% of the aggregate amount invested. There is no longer a $10,000 cap.

A shelter that registers with the IRS receives a registration number that the shelter then furnishes to its investors. A shelter investor who fails to include the registration number on Form 8271 and submit Form 8271 with the investor's tax return is subject to a penalty, unless there is reasonable cause for the failure to report the number.

The new law increases the penalty from $50 to $250. The increased penalty applies to returns filed after the date that President Reagan signed the Tax Reform Act.

Yet another penalty applies when a shelter organizer or seller fails to maintain a list of investors in a potentially abusive shelter, unless the failure is due to reasonable cause. The penalty remains $50 for each name missing from the list, but the Act increases the maximum annual penalty from $50,000 to $100,000.

The increased penalties for failure to register a shelter or to maintain an investor list became effective on the date that President Reagan signed the Act.

REPORTING TAX-EXEMPT INTEREST ON TAX RETURNS

The Tax Reform Act expands the existing obligation of individuals with taxable Social Security benefits to report the tax-exempt interest that they receive on their 1040 Forms. Starting with returns required to be filed for taxable years beginning after 1986 (Form 1040 for 1987 for individuals), all taxpayers, whether individuals, corporate or other, must report the tax-exempt interest that they receive.

EXTRA REQUIREMENT FOR CLAIMING DEPENDENCY DEDUCTION

The new law requires a taxpayer who files a Form 1040 on which he or she claims a dependency exemption for someone who is at least five years old to obtain a Social Security card for the dependent and to report the dependent's Social

Security number on the return. This requirement applies starting with returns for 1987 that are filed in 1988. There is a $5 penalty for failing to comply.

Why does the IRS want this information? Mainly to stop divorced or separated parents from both claiming the same child as an exemption.

Religious exemption. There is an exemption from the reporting requirement for members of religious groups that are exempt from the Social Security laws.

REPORTING SALES OF HOMES AND OTHER REAL ESTATE

Previously enacted legislation requires brokers to report the gross proceeds of sales of stocks, commodities, etc., on Form 1099 information returns with the IRS. The Tax Reform Act expands the reporting obligation to sales of real estate. Starting in 1987, one of the participants in a real estate transfer also must report the sale of that real estate, including a single-family home—a change that increases the ability of the IRS to check on whether sellers report gains.

Person in charge of closing the transaction is responsible for sending a Form 1099 to the IRS. The responsibility for listing a sale on a Form 1099 falls upon a number of participants in a descending order of responsibility. For reporting purposes, this means that the first person responsible for reporting is the person (including any attorney or title company) responsible for the closing. Generally, that is the person conducting the settlement. Congress has told the IRS to issue guidelines on who is the person responsible, as it may be unclear which of several persons involved with the closing is the one with primary responsibility for submitting a Form 1099. In the absence of that person, the responsibility then passes to the mortgage lender (the primary lender if more than one), then to the seller's real estate broker, then to the buyer's real estate broker (including a representative or agent), and finally, the person designated in IRS regulations.

Sales of single-family homes. In the past, if you sold your principal, that is, year-round residence, the only "notice" to the IRS might be your new address on Form 1040. This would be so if you failed to submit Schedule D, used when there is a taxable gain, or Form 2119, used when a home seller (1) postpones tax on all or part of the gain by buying a replacement residence; (2)

elects the over-age-55 exclusion of up to $125,000; or (3) suffers a loss, which is nondeductible.

Co-op apartments. The expanded reporting requirements apply to "real estate transactions." A question to be resolved by the IRS guidelines is whether a literal reading of the Tax Reform Act exempts sales of co-op apartments. The reason for the uncertainty is that the usual interest in a co-op is personal property; ownership is evidenced by a stock certificate that entitles the owner to occupy a certain apartment within a building and to use the common grounds. Odds are that there will be no exemption for co-op sales.

There is no uncertainty, though, for condo owners. They own real estate, in the same way as owners of single-family homes do.

REPORTING FEDERAL CONTRACT RECIPIENTS

To help the IRS track down unreported income, the new law requires Federal agencies to file information returns with the IRS on persons who receive Federal contracts. A return must state the name, address and identification number of a recipient and whatever other information IRS regulations may prescribe. The reporting requirement takes effect on January 1, 1987.

REPORTING ROYALTY PAYMENTS

The new law requires payers of royalties to report payments of $10 or more on Form 1099 information returns with the IRS, starting with payments made after 1986.

Types of royalties that must be reported. According to Congressional committee reports, they include payments with respect to the right to exploit natural resources, such as oil, gas, coal, timber, sand, gravel and other mineral interests, as well as payments for the right to exploit intangible property, such as copyrights, trade names, trademarks, books and other literary compositions, musical compositions, artistic works, secret processes or formulas and patents.

MAILINGS OF 1099 FORMS

The new law reduces mailing costs for corporations, banks and other payers of dividends, interest and royalties who have to send copies of Form 1099 information returns to the taxpayers who receive those payments. The revised rules allow corporations and other payers to include certain kinds of enclosures with their Form 1099 mailings, starting with mailings after the date that President Reagan signed the 1986 Tax Reform Act.

Other enclosures that accompany Form 1099 mailings. Payers can include only these three kinds of enclosures with a Form 1099 mailing: (1) a check; (2) a letter explaining why no check is enclosed, as when a company decides to skip a dividend payment; or (3) a statement of the taxpayer's specific account with the payer, such as a year-end summary of dividend payments by a corporation to a shareholder.

Statements on envelopes and enclosures. On the outside of the envelope for a 1099 Form mailing must appear the statement "Important Tax Return Document Enclosed." On each enclosure (the check, letter or account statement) must appear the statement "Important Tax Return Document Enclosed."

Impermissible enclosures. A 1099 Form mailing cannot be accompanied by such enclosures as advertising, promotional material or a quarterly or annual report. Those kinds of enclosures are impermissible, according to Congressional committee reports, because they may make it less likely that some taxpayers will recognize the importance of a Form 1099 and utilize it in completing their returns.

PASSPORT AND GREEN CARD APPLICATIONS

The Tax Reform Act requires information returns to be filed with the IRS by U.S. citizens residing abroad when they apply for passports and by resident aliens when they apply for green cards (permanent resident visas). The information returns will ask for such information as an individual's taxpayer identification number, a passport applicant's foreign country of residence and whether a green card applicant has had to file a tax return.

A person who fails to file the required information return is subject to a $500 penalty. The new requirement applies generally to passport and green card applications filed after 1987.

WITHHOLDING ON PENSION PAYMENTS OUTSIDE THE UNITED STATES

Generally, the law requires taxes to be withheld by corporations and other payers of pensions, IRA distributions and similar payments. Payers are relieved of the withholding requirement if a recipient elects to claim an exemption from withholding.

The new law tightens the withholding requirements for pension payments sent outside of the United States. The election to forego withholding is no longer available for such payments. Instead, a payer has to withhold unless the recipient certifies that he or she is not a U.S. citizen who resides overseas or a tax-avoidance expatriate. The new withholding requirement applies to payments after 1986.

RECOVERY OF ATTORNEY'S FEES IN TAX CASES FROM GOVERNMENT

The Tax Reform Act makes permanent a law that authorizes awards of reasonable attorney's fees in tax cases. Also, the new law eliminates the previous $25,000 cap on such awards, and substitutes a $75 an hour limitation, unless the court determines that a higher rate is justified.

The new law applies to amounts paid after September 30, 1986, in civil actions or proceedings commenced after 1985.

AUDIT DEADLINE EXTENDED BY THIRD-PARTY RECORDS DISPUTE

The law imposes a deadline, known as a statute of limitations, for the IRS to audit a return. As a general rule, the deadline is three years from the due date for the taxpayer's return.

The statute of limitations continues to run even if the IRS has to obtain records held by third parties, such as banks and other financial institutions that do business with the taxpayer. A problem arises when there is a dispute between the IRS and a third-party recordkeeper over access to those records. The statute could expire before there is a final determination on whether the IRS is entitled to those records, though the statute is suspended when the taxpayer intervenes in such a dispute.

The new law authorizes a suspension whether or not the taxpayer intervenes. Where the IRS issues a summons to a third party to turn certain records over to the IRS and six months elapse with an IRS versus third party dispute still unresolved, the statute is suspended until the dispute becomes resolved.

The third-party recordkeeper may have to notify the taxpayer whose records are the subject of the dispute of the statute suspension. The third party has to assume that chore when the IRS issues what is known as a "John Doe" summons, that is, a summons that demands certain records, but does not identify the taxpayer by name. The third party's failure to notify the taxpayer does not stop a statute suspension.

The new rule became effective on the date that President Reagan signed the Tax Reform Act.

RESCINDING STATUTORY NOTICE OF DEFICIENCY

Taxpayers can take disputes to the Tax Court only if the IRS issues a statutory notice of deficiency, also known as a 90-day letter. Under prior law, a notice cannot be withdrawn once it is issued. The new law permits withdrawal of the notice, provided the IRS and the taxpayer both agree to its withdrawal. The change applies retroactively to notices issued after 1985.

IRS CANNOT LEVY ON SERVICE-CONNECTED DISABILITY PAYMENTS

The IRS can seize assets to collect delinquent taxes. There is, though, an exemption from an IRS levy for various kinds of payments, including certain types of pensions. The new law adds military service connected disability payments to the list of assets that the IRS cannot seize. The change applies to payments made after 1986.

SPOUSES OF VIETNAM MIAs

The new law retroactively reinstates four tax relief provisions that apply to families of members of the U.S. armed forces missing in Vietnam. The provisions, which expired on December 31, 1982, will apply to all taxable years beginning after that date. The four provisions do the following:

(1) For purposes of defining a surviving spouse (for filing status purposes), the date of death or a person in MIA status is the date on which the determination of death is made.

(2) The income of an MIA who died in MIA status is exempt from income tax for the year in which the determination of death is made and any prior year that ends after the first day the MIA served in a combat zone.

(3) The spouse of a person in MIA status can elect to file a joint return.

(4) The rules postponing the performing of certain acts by reason of service in a combat zone apply to spouses of MIAs. Those acts include filing returns and paying taxes.

INFORMATION SHARING BY IRS WITH CITIES

The IRS now shares tax information with states. The new law expands the sharing to cities with populations of over two million. The change became effective on the date that President Reagan signed the Tax Reform Act.

RETURN-FREE FILING SYSTEM

Congress wants the IRS to determine whether it is possible to use computers to develop a return-free system for individuals that eases the paperwork burden for the IRS and relieves many persons of the annual filing chore.

APPENDIX A

THE NEW LAW'S EFFECT ON REPRESENTATIVE HOUSEHOLDS

Although it is difficult to generalize about the new law's effect on taxpayers, one thing is clear from the examples that follow: Taxes are not cut across the board for all taxpayers. Some will find an increase in their tax bills. Others will stay just about where they were under the old law. The examples that follow reflect all new-law provisions and phase-ins that apply to individuals and assume the same dollar amount of income and gross expenses in each year.

Use the worksheet on the following pages to determine your comparative tax bills for 1986, 1987, and 1988.

I. Worksheet for Comparing Your Tax Liability

	1986	1987	1988
Taxpayer's salary			
Spouse's salary			
Interest			
Taxable dividends			
Taxable portion of long-term capital gains			
Gross income (loss) from business, practice, shelters, etc.			
GROSS INCOME			
IRA deduction			
2-earner deduction			
ADJUSTED GROSS INCOME (AGI)			
Nonitemizers charitable deduction			
Old personal exemptions			
Excess itemized deductions			
New personal exemptions			
New standard deduction			
Total itemized deductions (from Itemized Deduction Chart)			
TAXABLE INCOME			
TAX PAYABLE			

II. Itemized Deductions

	1986	1987	1988
(1) Total medical expenses	_____	_____	_____
(2) "Floor"	_____	_____	_____
(3) Net medical deduction Items (1-2)	_____	_____	_____
(4) State and local income taxes	_____	_____	_____
(5) Real estate taxes	_____	_____	_____
(6) Sales taxes	_____	_____	_____
(7) Other taxes	_____	_____	_____
(8) Home mortgage interest	_____	_____	_____
(9) Credit card interest and other loan interest	_____	_____	_____
(10) Charitable contributions	_____	_____	_____
(11) Total miscellaneous deductions	_____	_____	_____
(12) "Floor"	_____	_____	_____
(13) Net miscellaneous deductions	_____	_____	_____
(14) Total itemized deductions (3) through (10) + (13)	_____	_____	_____
(15) Zero bracket amount	_____	_____	_____
(16) Excess itemized deductions Items (14 − 15)	_____	_____	_____

CASE 1: MARTHA SIMMONS

Martha Simmons is a single taxpayer with $12,000 of salary income and $100 of dividend income. She does not make an IRA contribution and has no charitable contributions. Martha is a renter.

Tax for 1986 — $1,197, close to 10% of her gross income.
Tax for 1987 — $1,077, about 9% of her gross income. Her tax is roughly 10% lower than in 1986.
Tax for 1988 — $1,072.

Martha benefits from a higher personal exemption ($1,900 in 1987, and $1,950 in 1988, as opposed to $1,080 in 1986), and a bigger standard deduction ($2,540 in 1987, and $3,000 in 1988, versus $2,480 zero bracket amount (ZBA) in 1986).

Case 1: Martha Simmons

	1986	1987	1988
Taxpayer's salary	12,000	12,000	12,000
Spouse's salary	N/A	N/A	N/A
Interest	100	100	100
Taxable dividends	-0-	-0-	-0-
Taxable portion of long-term capital gains	-0-	-0-	-0-
Gross income (loss) from business, practice, shelters, etc.	-0-	-0-	-0-
GROSS INCOME	12,100	12,100	12,100
IRA deduction	-0-	-0-	-0-
2-earner deduction	N/A	N/A	N/A
ADJUSTED GROSS INCOME (AGI)	12,100	12,100	12,100
Nonitemizers charitable deduction	-0-	N/A	N/A
Old personal exemptions	(1,080)	N/A	N/A
Excess itemized deductions	N/A	N/A	N/A
New personal exemptions	N/A	(1,900)	(1,950)
New standard deduction	N/A	(2,540)	(3,000)
Total itemized deductions (from Itemized Deduction Chart)	N/A	N/A	N/A
TAXABLE INCOME	11,020	7,660	7,150
TAX PAYABLE	1,197	1,077	1,072
ITEMIZED DEDUCTIONS	N/A	N/A	N/A

CASE 2: TED AND ANNE BENSON

Ted and Anne Benson, ages 66, are retired. They have $15,000 of income from Ted's pension, $2,000 of interest income, and $10,000 of Social Security benefits. They own their home free and clear. They have $3,000 of unreimbursed medical expenses, $400 of charitable contributions, $400 of credit card interest, $2,000 of property taxes, $100 of state income tax, $200 of sales tax, and $150 of miscellaneous itemized deductions (tax return preparation fee, safe deposit box, etc.). Because their income does not exceed a statutory level, the Benson's do not owe a federal tax on their Social Security benefits in 1986, 1987, or 1988.

Tax for 1986 — $ 906, about 5% of their income exclusive of Social Security
Tax for 1987 — $ 930, an increase of $24.
Tax for 1988 — $1,035, an increase of $129 over their 1986 bill.

Basic reasons for the increase: Although taxable income drops in 1987 and 1988, more of the income is subject to a higher marginal tax.

Case 2: Ted and Anne Benson

	1986	1987	1988
Taxpayer's pension	15,000	15,000	15,000
Spouse's pension	-0-	-0-	-0-
Interest	2,000	2,000	2,000
Taxable dividends	-0-	-0-	-0-
Taxable portion of long-term capital gains	-0-	-0-	-0-
Gross income (loss) from business, practice, shelters, etc.	-0-	-0-	-0-
GROSS INCOME	17,000	17,000	17,000
IRA deduction	N/A	N/A	N/A
2-earner deduction	N/A	N/A	N/A
ADJUSTED GROSS INCOME (AGI)	17,000	17,000	17,000
Nonitemizers charitable deduction	N/A	N/A	N/A
Old personal exemptions	(4,320)	N/A	N/A
Excess itemized deductions	(1,730)	N/A	N/A
New personal exemptions	N/A	(3,800)	(3,900)
New standard deduction	N/A	(6,200)	(6,200)
Total itemized deductions (from Itemized Deduction Chart)	N/A	N/A	N/A
TAXABLE INCOME	10,950	7,000	6,900
TAX PAYABLE	906	930	1,035

II. Itemized Deductions	1986	1987	1988
(1) Total medical expenses	3,000		
(2) "Floor"	(850)		
(3) Net medical deduction Items (1-2)	2,150		
(4) State and local income taxes	100		
(5) Real estate taxes	2,000		
(6) Sales taxes	200		
(7) Other taxes	-0-		
(8) Home mortgage interest	-0-		
(9) Credit card interest and other loan interest	400		
(10) Charitable contributions	400		
(11) Total miscellaneous deductions	150		
(12) "Floor"	-0-		
(13) Net miscellaneous deductions (11 − 12)	150		
(14) Total itemized deductions (3) through (10) + (13)	5,400		
(15) Zero bracket amount	(3,670)		
(16) Excess itemized deductions Items (14 − 15)	1,730		

CASE 3: ROBERT AND BETH KAHN

Robert Kahn earns $25,000 a year; his wife, Beth, earns $10,000. They have $350 of interest income and Robert has been putting $500 into his IRA each year. They make $400 of charitable contributions. The Kahns are renters who do not itemize their deductions. They have no children.

Tax for 1986 — $4,925, about 14% of their gross income.
Tax for 1987 — $3,967, a savings of $958. Their tax is about 11.2% of their gross income.
Tax for 1988 — $3,892, a savings of $1,033 over their 1986 bill. Their tax bill is down to about 11% of their gross income.

The Kahns benefit in a big way from the increased standard deduction and personal exemptions and from lower tax rates. The only tax break they lose is the deduction for two-earner couples.

Case 3: Robert and Beth Kahn

	1986	1987	1988
Taxpayer's salary	25,000	25,000	25,000
Spouse's salary	10,000	10,000	10,000
Interest	350	350	350
Taxable dividends	-0-	-0-	-0-
Taxable portion of long-term capital gains	-0-	-0-	-0-
Gross income (loss) from business, practice, shelters, etc.	-0-	-0-	-0-
GROSS INCOME	35,350	35,350	35,350
IRA deduction	(500)	(500)	(500)
2-earner deduction	(1,000)	N/A	N/A
ADJUSTED GROSS INCOME (AGI)	33,850	33,850	33,850
Nonitemizers charitable deduction	(400)	N/A	N/A
Old personal exemptions	(2,100)	N/A	N/A
Excess itemized deductions	N/A	N/A	N/A
New personal exemptions	N/A	(3,800)	(3,900)
New standard deduction	N/A	(3,800)	(5,000)
Total itemized deductions (from Itemized Deduction Chart)	N/A	N/A	N/A
TAXABLE INCOME	31,290	27,250	25,950
TAX PAYABLE	4,925	3,967	3,892

CASE 4: CHARLES AND BETTY CRANE

Charles Crane earns $35,000 in salary; his wife, Betty, earns $15,000. They have $500 of interest income. Charles, who is covered by his company retirement plan, has been making a $1,000 IRA contribution each year. The Cranes have one child. Their expenses are as follows: $1,500, unreimbursed doctor bills; $1,200, state income tax; $2,300, property tax; $345, sales tax; $4,000, home mortgage interest; $2,000, credit card interest and car loan interest; $300, charitable contributions; and $140, miscellaneous itemized deductions.

Tax for 1986 — $6,823, roughly 13.5% of their gross income.
Tax for 1987 — $6,236, a savings of $587. The tax is about 12.3% of their gross income.
Tax for 1988 — $6,226, which is $597 less than the 1986 bill. The tax is about 12.3% of their gross income.

The Cranes lose their IRA deduction and the deduction for two-earner spouses. But the substantial boost in personal exemptions and the standard deduction, and the lower tax rates, more than make up for the loss of these two tax breaks.

Case 4: Charles and Betty Crane

	1986	1987	1988
Taxpayer's salary	35,000	35,000	35,000
Spouse's salary	15,000	15,000	15,000
Interest	500	500	500
Taxable dividends	-0-	-0-	-0-
Taxable portion of long-term capital gains	-0-	-0-	-0-
Gross income (loss) from business, practice, shelters, etc.	-0-	-0-	-0-
GROSS INCOME	50,500	50,500	50,500
IRA deduction	(1,000)	-0-	-0-
2-earner deduction	(1,500)	N/A	N/A
ADJUSTED GROSS INCOME (AGI)	48,000	50,500	50,500
Nonitemizers charitable deduction	N/A	N/A	N/A
Old personal exemptions	(3,240)	N/A	N/A
Excess itemized deductions	(6,615)	N/A	N/A
New personal exemptions	N/A	(5,700)	(5,850)
New standard deduction	N/A	N/A	N/A
Total itemized deductions from Itemized Deduction Chart)	N/A	(9,100)	(8,600)
TAXABLE INCOME	38,145	35,700	36,050
TAX PAYABLE	6,823	6,236	6,226

II. Itemized Deductions	1986	1987	1988
(1) Total medical expenses	1,500	1,500	1,500
(2) "Floor"	(2,400)	(3,787)	(3,787)
(3) Net medical deduction Items (1-2)	-0-	-0-	-0-
(4) State and local income taxes	1,200	1,200	1,200
(5) Real estate taxes	2,300	2,300	2,300
(6) Sales taxes	345	-0-	-0-
(7) Other taxes	-0-	-0-	-0-
(8) Home mortgage interest	4,000	4,000	4,000
(9) Credit card interest and other loan interest	2,000	1,300	800
(10) Charitable contributions	300	300	300
(11) Total miscellaneous deductions	140	140	140
(12) "Floor"	-0-	(1,010)	(1,010)
(13) Net miscellaneous deductions	140	-0-	-0-
(14) Total itemized deductions (3) through (10) + (13)	10,285	9,100	8,600
(15) Zero bracket amount	(3,670)	N/A	N/A
(16) Excess itemized deductions Items (14 − 15)	6,615	N/A	N/A

CASE 5: RICHARD AND PATRICIA ABLE

Richard Able earns $40,000 in salary; his wife, Patricia, earns $25,000. Richard is covered by his employer's profit sharing plan. They have $800 of interest income and $400 of dividend income. Richard, an avid stock market investor, has been pulling down about $4,000 in long-term capital gains each year. The Ables have been putting away $2,500 each year in an IRA account ($1,250 from each spouse). The Cranes have the following expenses: $1,800, state income tax; $3,000, real estate tax; $410, sales tax; $7,000, home mortgage interest; $1,000, credit card interest; $600, charitable contributions; and $300 of miscellaneous expenses (tax return preparation, safe deposit box, etc.). The Ables have two children, ages 9 and 10.

Tax for 1986 — $10,022, roughly 15% of their gross income.
Tax for 1987 — $10,152, a $130 increase.
Tax for 1988 — $10,020, $2 less than their 1986 tax bill.

The Ables are more or less in the same position as they were before the new law. The benefits of higher personal exemptions and lower rates are offset by the higher tax on their long-term capital gains. Without capital gains in the picture, their tax bill would drop from $9,494 in 1986, to $9,032 in 1987, and to $8,900 in 1988.

Now, let's add a few facts and assume each of the Able children has $1,000 of interest income from bank accounts established in their name by their parents. For 1986, the children don't pay any tax on their income since the interest is offset by the $1,080 personal exemption that each child is entitled to claim. Beginning in 1987, however, each child loses the personal exemption if he or she can be claimed as a dependent by a parent. The first $500 of a child's unearned income can be sheltered from tax with the standard deduction. However, the excess over $500 is taxed. On our facts, the total 1987 tax bill on the children's income is $110; for 1988, the total tax bill on the children's income is $150.

Case 5: Richard and Patricia Able

	1986	1987	1988
Taxpayer's salary	40,000	40,000	40,000
Spouse's salary	25,000	25,000	25,000
Interest	800	800	800
Taxable dividends	200	400	400
Taxable portion of long-term capital gains	1,600	4,000	4,000
Gross income (loss) from business, practice, shelters, etc.	-0-	-0-	-0-
GROSS INCOME	67,600	70,200	70,200
IRA deduction	(2,500)	N/A	N/A
2-earner deduction	(2,500)	N/A	N/A
ADJUSTED GROSS INCOME (AGI)	62,600	70,200	70,200
Nonitemizers charitable deduction	N/A	N/A	N/A
Old personal exemptions	(4,320)	N/A	N/A
Excess itemized deductions	(10,440)	N/A	N/A
New personal exemptions	N/A	(7,600)	(7,800)
New standard deduction	N/A	N/A	N/A
Total itemized deductions (from Itemized Deduction Chart)	N/A	(13,050)	(12,800)
TAXABLE INCOME	47,840	49,550	49,600
TAX PAYABLE	10,022	10,152	10,020

II. Itemized Deductions	1986	1987	1988
(1) Total medical expenses	-0-	-0-	-0-
(2) "Floor"	-0-	-0-	-0-
(3) Net medical deduction Items (1-2)	-0-	-0-	-0-
(4) State and local income taxes	1,800	1,800	1,800
(5) Real estate taxes	3,000	3,000	3,000
(6) Sales taxes	410	-0-	-0-
(7) Other taxes	-0-	-0-	-0-
(8) Home mortgage interest	7,000	7,000	7,000
(9) Credit card interest and other loan interest	1,000	650	400
(10) Charitable contributions	600	600	600
(11) Total miscellaneous deductions	300	300	300
(12) "Floor"	-0-	(1,404)	(1,404)
(13) Net miscellaneous deductions	300	-0-	-0-
(14) Total itemized deductions (3) through (10) + (13)	14,110	13,050	12,800
(15) Zero bracket amount	(3,670)	N/A	N/A
(16) Excess itemized deductions Items (14 − 15)	10,440	N/A	N/A

CASE 6: CARL AND RHONDA JEFFERSON

Carl and Rhonda Jefferson are empty nesters in their 50's. Carl, a high-level executive, earns $130,000 in salary, and is covered by the company's retirement plan. Rhonda is a homemaker. The Jeffersons have $3,000 of interest income and $2,000 of dividend income. Each year, they have about $10,000 in long-term gains from the sale of stock; they also also invest in tax shelters that produce a $25,000 annual net loss. Carl has been making a $2,250 IRA contribution each year. Their expenses are as follows: $6,000, state income tax; $5,000, property tax; $418, sales tax; $14,000, home mortgage interest; $3,000, credit-card interest; $1,800, charitable contributions; $800, miscellaneous itemized deductions.

Tax bill for 1986 — $23,632, about 21% of their gross income.
Tax bill for 1987 — $32,183, an $8,551 boost.
Tax bill for 1988 — $29,860, which is $6,228 more than the bill for 1986.

The Jeffersons wind up paying more because they lose many of their tax breaks. The long-term capital gains exclusion disappears in 1987, and the Jeffersons can't use the $25,000 of loss from their shelters to offset their income.

Case 6: Carl and Rhonda Jefferson

	1986	1987	1988
Taxpayer's salary	130,000	130,000	130,000
Spouse's salary	-0-	-0-	-0-
Interest	3,000	3,000	3,000
Taxable dividends	1,800	2,000	2,000
Taxable portion of long-term capital gains	4,000	10,000	10,000
Gross income (loss) from business, practice, shelters, etc.	(25,000)	-0-	-0-
GROSS INCOME	113,800	145,000	145,000
IRA deduction	(2,250)	N/A	N/A
2-earner deduction	N/A	N/A	N/A
ADJUSTED GROSS INCOME (AGI)	111,550	145,000	145,000
Nonitemizers charitable deduction	N/A	N/A	N/A
Old personal exemptions	(2,160)	N/A	N/A
Excess itemized deductions	(27,348)	N/A	N/A
New personal exemptions	N/A	(3,800)	(3,900)
New standard deduction	N/A	N/A	N/A
Total itemized deductions from Itemized Deduction Chart)	N/A	(28,750)	(28,000)
TAXABLE INCOME	82,042	112,450	113,100
TAX PAYABLE	23,632	32,183	29,860

II. Itemized Deductions	1986	1987	1988
(1) Total medical expenses	-0-	-0-	-0-
(2) "Floor"	-0-	-0-	-0-
(3) Net medical deduction Items (1-2)	-0-	-0-	-0-
(4) State and local income taxes	6,000	6,000	6,000
(5) Real estate taxes	5,000	5,000	5,000
(6) Sales taxes	418	-0-	-0-
(7) Other taxes	-0-	-0-	-0-
(8) Home mortgage interest	14,000	14,000	14,000
(9) Credit card interest and other loan interest	3,000	1,950	1,200
(10) Charitable contributions	1,800	1,800	1,800
(11) Total miscellaneous deductions	800	800	800
(12) "Floor"	-0-	(2,900)	(2,900)
(13) Net miscellaneous deductions	800	-0-	-0-
(14) Total itemized deductions (3) through (10) + (13)	31,018	28,750	28,000
(15) Zero bracket amount	(3,670)	N/A	N/A
(16) Excess itemized deductions Items (14 − 15)	27,348	N/A	N/A

CASE 7: HART SANDERSON

Hart Sanderson, a divorced taxpayer, is an attorney with a Wall Street firm. He earns $180,000 each year in salary and bonuses, plus $8,000 in interest income. He's so busy that he hasn't taken the time to invest in tax shelters or even to buy a home. Hart has been making a $2,000 IRA contribution each year, but he'll lose this break in 1987 since he's covered by his firm's retirement plan. Hart rents an apartment. His expenses: $30,000, deductible alimony; $7,000, state income tax; $418, sales tax; $2,000, charitable contributions; and $500, miscellaneous expenses.

Tax bill for 1986 — $60,722, about 32% of his gross income.
Tax bill for 1987 — $50,597, a huge savings of $10,125 over 1986.
Tax bill for 1988 — $41,720. Hart pays $19,002 less than in 1986, an incredible windfall. Now, his tax is roughly 22% of his gross income.

Hart is a big winner because of the reduction in the top marginal tax rates. In 1986, more than $59,000 of his taxable income was taxed at the 50% rate. In 1988, he'll be paying a flat tax of 28% on his taxable income, plus a surcharge of $546 (this eliminates the tax benefit of claiming a personal exemption).

Case 7: Hart Sanderson

	1986	1987	1988
Taxpayer's salary	180,000	180,000	180,000
Spouse's salary	-0-	-0-	-0-
Interest	8,000	8,000	8,000
Taxable dividends	-0-	-0-	-0-
Taxable portion of long-term capital gains	-0-	-0-	-0-
Gross income (loss) from business, practice, shelters, etc.	-0-	-0-	-0-
GROSS INCOME	188,000	188,000	188,000
IRA deduction	(2,000)	N/A	N/A
Deductible alimony	(30,000)	(30,000)	(30,000)
ADJUSTED GROSS INCOME (AGI)	156,000	158,000	158,000
Nonitemizers charitable deduction	N/A	N/A	N/A
Old personal exemptions	(1,080)	N/A	N/A
Excess itemized deductions	(7,438)	N/A	N/A
New personal exemptions	N/A	(1,900)	(1,950)
New standard deduction	N/A	N/A	N/A
Total itemized deductions (from Itemized Deduction Chart)	N/A	(9,000)	(9,000)
TAXABLE INCOME	147,482	147,100	147,050
TAX PAYABLE	60,722	50,597	41,720

II. Itemized Deductions	1986	1987	1988
(1) Total medical expenses	-0-	-0-	-0-
(2) "Floor"	-0-	-0-	-0-
(3) Net medical deduction Items (1-2)	-0-	-0-	-0-
(4) State and local income taxes	7,000	7,000	7,000
(5) Real estate taxes	-0-	-0-	-0-
(6) Sales taxes	418	-0-	-0-
(7) Other taxes	-0-	-0-	-0-
(8) Home mortgage interest	-0-	-0-	-0-
(9) Credit card interest and other loan interest	-0-	-0-	-0-
(10) Charitable contributions	2,000	2,000	2,000
(11) Total miscellaneous deductions	500	500	500
(12) "Floor"	-0-	(3,160)	(3,160)
(13) Net miscellaneous deductions	500	-0-	-0-
(14) Total itemized deductions (3) through (10) + (13)	9,918	9,000	9,000
(15) Zero bracket amount	(2,480)	N/A	N/A
(16) Excess itemized deductions Items (14 − 15)	7,438	N/A	N/A

APPENDIX B

TAX TABLES—TAX YEAR 1986

(NOTE: For estimating purposes, use these rate schedules, although for your 1986 return you should use special IRS tables for taxable incomes under $50,000.)

Chart A
Married Filing Joint Returns
and Qualifying Widows and Widowers

If taxable income* is:		The tax is:	of the amount
Over—	but not over—		over—
$0	$3,670	-0-	
3,670	5,940	...... 11%	$3,670
5,940	8,200	$249.70 + 12%	5,940
8,200	12,840	520.90 + 14%	8,200
12,840	17,270	1,170.50 + 16%	12,840
17,270	21,800	1,879.30 + 18%	17,270
21,800	26,550	2,694.70 + 22%	21,800
26,550	32,270	3,739.70 + 25%	26,550
32,270	37,980	5,169.70 + 28%	32,270
37,980	49,420	6,768.50 + 33%	37,980
49,420	64,750	10,543.70 + 38%	49,420
64,750	92,370	16,369.10 + 42%	64,750
92,370	118,050	27,969.50 + 45%	92,370
118,050	175,250	39,525.50 + 49%	118,050
175,250	———	67,553.50 + 50%	175,250

Chart B
Married Filing Separate Returns

If taxable income* is:		The tax is:	of the amount over—
Over—	but not over—		
$0	$1,835	-0-	
1,835	2,970	...... 11%	$1,835
2,970	4,100	$124.85 + 12%	2,970
4,100	6,420	260.45 + 14%	4,100
6,420	8,635	585.25 + 16%	6,420
8,635	10,900	939.65 + 18%	8,635
10,900	13,275	1,347.35 + 22%	10,900
13,275	16,135	1,869.85 + 25%	13,275
16,135	18,990	2,584.85 + 28%	16,135
18,900	24,710	3,384.25 + 33%	18,990
24,710	32,375	5,271.85 + 38%	24,710
32,375	46,185	8,184.55 + 42%	32,375
46,185	59,025	13,984.75 + 45%	46,185
59,025	87,625	19,762.75 + 49%	59,025

Chart C
Single Taxpayers

If taxable income* is:		The tax is:	of the amount over—
Over—	but not over—		
$0	$2,480	-0-	
2,480	3,670	...... 11%	$2,480
3,670	4,750	$130.90 + 12%	3,670
4,750	7,010	260.50 + 14%	4,750
7,010	9,170	576.90 + 15%	7,010
9,170	11,650	900.90 + 16%	9,170
11,650	13,920	1,297.70 + 18%	11,650
13,920	16,190	1,706.30 + 20%	13,920
16,190	19,640	2,160.30 + 23%	16,190
19,640	25,360	2,953.80 + 26%	19,640
25,360	31,080	4,441.00 + 30%	25,360
31,080	36,800	6,157.00 + 34%	31,080
36,800	44,780	8,101.80 + 38%	36,800
44,780	59,670	11,134.20 + 42%	44,780
59,670	88,270	17,388.00 + 48%	59,670
88,270	------	31,116.00 + 50%	88,270

Chart D
Heads of Household

| If taxable income* is: | | The tax is: | of the amount |
Over—	but not over—		over—
$0	$2,480	-0-	
2,480	4,750	...... 11%	$2,480
4,750	7,010	$249.70 + 12%	4,750
7,010	9,390	520.90 + 14%	7,010
9,390	12,730	854.10 + 17%	9,390
12,730	16,190	1,421.90 + 18%	12,730
16,190	19,640	2,044.70 + 20%	16,190
19,640	25,360	2,734.70 + 24%	19,640
25,360	31,080	4,107.50 + 28%	25,360
31,080	36,800	5,709.10 + 32%	31,080
36,800	48,240	7,539.50 + 35%	36,800
48,240	65,390	11,543.50 + 42%	48,240
65,390	88,270	18,746.50 + 45%	65,390
88,270	116,870	29,042.50 + 48%	88,270
116,870	-------	42,770.50 + 50%	116,870

*Taxable income is found as follows: (1) Combine income and loss items—e.g., compensation, bonuses, net income or loss from trade or business, taxed portion of long-term capital gains, up to $3,000 of net losses from sale of assets such as securities (long-term loss offsets income on a two-for-one basis)—to arrive at gross income. (2) Subtract adjustments (moving expenses, certain employee business expenses, IRA deduction, deduction for two-earner couples) to arrive at adjusted gross income (AGI). (3) Non-itemizers subtract personal exemptions and charitable contribution from AGI. The result is taxable income. Itemizers subtract personal exemptions and excess itemized deductions (EID) to arrive at taxable income. EID is the excess of total itemized deductions over the zero bracket amount of $3,670 on your return; $2,480 for single and head of household, and $1,835 for married filing separately.

TAX TABLES—TAX YEAR 1987

Chart A
Married Filing Joint Returns
and Qualifying Widows and Widowers

| If taxable income* is: | | The tax is: | of the amount |
Over—	but not over—		over—
$0	$3,000	...... 11%	$0
13,000	28,000	$330.00 + 15%	3,000
28,000	45,000	4,080.00 + 28%	28,000
45,000	90,000	8,840.00 + 35%	45,000
90,000	------	24,590.00 + 38.5%	90,000

Chart B
Married Filing Separate Returns

| If taxable income* is: | | The tax is: | of the amount |
Over—	but not over—		over—
$0	$1,500	...... 11%	$0
1,500	14,000	$165.00 + 15%	1,500
14,000	22,500	2,040.00 + 28%	14,000
22,500	45,000	4,420.00 + 35%	22,500
45,000	------	12,295.00 + 38.5%	45,000

Chart C
Single Taxpayers

If taxable income* is:		The tax is:	of the amount over–
Over–	but not over–		
$0	$1,800	...... 11%	$0
1,800	16,800	$198.00 + 15%	1,800
16,800	27,000	2,448.00 + 28%	16,800
27,000	54,000	5,304.00 + 35%	27,000
54,000	------	14,754.00 + 38.5%	54,000

Chart D
Heads of Households

If taxable income* is:		The tax is:	of the amount over–
Over–	but not over–		
$0	$2,500	...... 11%	$0
2,500	23,000	$275.00 + 15%	2,500
23,000	38,000	3,350.00 + 28%	23,000
38,000	80,000	7,550.00 + 35%	38,000
80,000	------	22,250.00 + 38.5%	80,000

*Taxable income is found as follows: (1) Combine income and loss items—e.g., compensation, bonuses, net income or loss from trade or business, long-term capital gains, up to $3,000 from sale of assets such as securities— to arrive at gross income. (2) Subtract adjustments (e.g., certain reimbursed employee business expenses and IRA deduction, if you qualify) to arrive at adjusted gross income (AGI). (3) Non-itemizers substract personal exemptions and the standard deduction from AGI. The result is taxable income. Itemizers subtract personal exemptions and total of itemized deductions to arrive at taxable income.

Note: For 1987, long-term capital gains are taxed at a maximum rate of 28%. So if the taxpayer's top tax rate exceeds 28%, the tax on long-term capital gains is figured seperately from the tax on other income.

TAX TABLES—TAX YEAR 1988

Chart A
Married Filing Joint Returns
and Qualifying Widows and Widowers

If taxable income* is: Over–	but not over–	The tax is:	of the amount over–
$0	$29,750	...... 15%	$0
29,750	71,900	$4,462.50 + 28%	29,750
71,900	149,250	16,264.50 + 33%**	71,900
149,250	-------	...... 28%***	$0

Chart B
Married Filing Separate Returns

If taxable income* is: Over–	but not over–	The tax is:	of the amount over–
$0	$14,875	...... 15%	$0
14,875	35,950	$2,231.25 + 28%	14,875
35,950	113,300	8,132.25 + 33%**	35,950
113,300	-------	...... 28%***	$0

Chart C
Single Taxpayers

If taxable income* is: Over—	but not over—	The tax is:	of the amount over—
$0	$17,850	...... 15%	$0
17,850	43,150	$2,677.50 + 28%	17,850
43,150	89,560	9,761.50 + 33%**	43,150
89,560	------	...... 28%***	$0

Chart D
Heads of Household

If taxable income* is: Over—	but not over—	The tax is:	of the amount over—
$0	$23,900	...... 15%	$0
23,900	61,650	$3,585.00 + 28%	23,900
61,650	123,790	14,155.00 + 33%	61,650
123,790	------	...... 28%	$0

*Taxable income is determined as follows: (1) Combine income and loss items (e.g., compensation, bonuses, net income or loss from trade or business, gain [or up to $3,000 of loss] from sales of securities). (2) Subtract adjustments (e.g., certain reimbursed employee business expenses and IRA deduction, if you qualify) to arrive at adjusted gross income (AGI). (3) Non-itemizers substract personal exemptions and the standard deduction from AGI. The result is taxable income. Itemizers subtract personal exemptions and total of itemized deductions to arrive at taxable income.

**Reflects 5% surtax which phases out benefit of having part of income taxed at 15% rate.

***Flat tax of 28% on all taxable income. To this figure, add 5% surtax which phases out tax benefit of exemptions. Surtax is the lesser of (a) 28% of the sum of personal and dependency exemptions, or (b) 5% of (taxable income — $149,250) on joint return; 5% of (taxable income — $89,560) on single return; 5% of (taxable income — $123,790) on head of household return; 5% of (taxable income — $113,300) on married filing a separate return.